The Day of the Dead

The Day of the Dead

When Two Worlds Meet in Oaxaca

Shawn D. Haley
&
Curt Fukuda

berghahn
NEW YORK · OXFORD
www.berghahnbooks.com

Published in 2004 by
Berghahn Books
www.berghahnbooks.com

©2004, 2006, 2014 Shawn D. Haley and Curt Fukuda
Reprinted in 2006 and 2014

Library of Congress Cataloging-in-Publication Data

Haley, Shawn D.
  The day of the dead : when two worlds meet in Oaxaca / Shawn D. Haley & Curt Fukuda.
    p. cm.
  Includes bibliographical references and index.
  ISBN 978-1-84545-083-0 (alk. paper)
   1. All Souls' Day--Mexico--Oaxaca de Juàrez. 2. Death--Symbolic
aspects--Mexico--Oaxaca de Juàrez. 3. Altars--Mexico--Oaxaca de Juàrez. 4.
Cemeteries--Mexico--Oaxaca de Juàrez. 5. Fasts and feasts--Mexico--Oaxaca de Juàrez.
6. Oaxaca de Juàrez (Mexico)--Religious life and customs. 7. Oaxaca de Juàrez.
(Mexico--Social life and customs. I. Fukuda, Curt. II. Title.

GT4995.A4H352003
394.264'0972'74–dc21 20033052191

British Library Cataloguing in Publication Data

A catalogue record for this book is available from the British Library

Printed on acid-free paper

ISBN: 978-1-84545-083-0 (paperback)
ISBN: 978-1-78238-608-7 (ebook)

Table of Contents

For Ellie & Monica & Our Families
&
All Our Oaxacan Friends

Acknowledgements

In 1996, Lucero Topete, the owner of the Instituto Cultural Oaxaca (a Spanish language school) and a good friend, suggested that Curt and I combine our efforts. I had been conducting research on the Day of the Dead with the intention of writing a book on the subject while Curt was taking a large number of photographs of the same subject. Lucero introduced us and we have been working together ever since. This book is the result of that collaboration. Thank you, Lucero, for the idea.

Many people had a hand in this work and we want to thank all of them. Of course, the project would not have even begun had not the people of Oaxaca opened their doors and their hearts to us. There are far too many to list here but we think of them often. But a few deserve special mention. Estela Gaona, Pedro Torres, Misael Vásquez, and Norma Martínez deserve special recognition for the help and support they so graciously gave us. We will forever be in their debt. Red Deer College and Eagle Valley Research Ltd. provided some funding for the project while the Instituto Cultural Oaxaca made us welcome and became our home base in Oaxaca.

Curt would also like to thank Russell Preston Brown, Son Do, Salvador and Colleen Gonzalez, Nina Vivian Huryn, Yolanda Johnson, Juan Luna, Hector and Dolores Manzano and family, Taka and Lolita Manzano-Kamezawa, Mary Jane Mendoza, Zacarias and Emilia Ruiz, Michael and Alice Salinero, David Sanchez, Cynthia Steele, Inocencio Velasco and family, Henry Wangeman and Rosa Blum, and William Ward. Special thanks go to Lissa Jones.

Additional photographs were provided by Lissa Jones, Monica Smith, and Ellie Braun-Haley. Thank you for letting us use the images. Thanks is also due to John Gledhill who reviewed the manuscript and whose insightful comments helped make it better.

Our spouses, Monica Smith and Ellie Braun-Haley, encouraged us and gave us the strength to forge ahead. They also made constructive editorial and design suggestions many of which have been incorporated into the final drafts. It is as much their project as it is ours. Thank you.

Shawn D. Haley

1. The Day of the Dead

The Aztec called the hummingbird the 'Messenger of the Gods' because this tiny bird seemed to exist in both the natural and the supernatural world at the same time. Its body was in our world while its wings, beating so fast as to be invisible, were in the other world. For most of the Mesoamerican peoples, including the Zapotec of central Oaxaca, there is a very fine line that separates the world of the living from the supernatural world where the dead live. On *el diá de muertos* (the Day of the Dead), that line dissolves and, for a time, there is only one world. At that time, November first and second, the dead return to their former homes on earth for a while to eat, to drink, to sing, to be entertained, and to visit with their loved ones. The dead return home as they have done for millennia and the living throw open their doors to them. The reunion is indeed joyous and is a time that is eagerly anticipated.

It is called the Day of the Dead but it is more like a 'season' of the dead. It begins in mid-October with a formal invitation issued by the living and continues until San Andreas Day (November 30) when, it is said, San Andreas closes the gates of Heaven after all of the souls have returned.[1] However,

An elaborate and irreverent Day of the Dead ofrenda built in the home of Juan Manuel, a silversmith in the city of Oaxaca.

1. Lechuga 2002.

most of the activity centers on the first two days of November, the Spanish Catholic All Saints' and All Souls' Days, but there is little of the Spanish influence to be found in the Oaxacan Day of the Dead. The Spanish version, which is bleak and dismal, requires one to go to the cemetery to pray and to mourn once again for lost loved ones. For the Oaxaqueñans, these days are not bleak and dismal, rather they are joyous and exuberant. It is not a mourning of lost loved ones, but a celebration, a reunion with the dead.

For many of the people of southern Mexico, the influence *el diá de muertos* has on their daily lives is immeasurable. It affects everything they do. It certainly has an impact on the way they see the world and themselves in it. For example, Soledad claimed that her home was in the tiny village of San Dionicio, despite the fact that she was born in Ocotlán and has never lived anywhere else. To her and to many others, home is not where you were born. It has nothing to do with where you live. It is where your dead are buried. Soledad's grandparents are buried in San Dionicio and so that is 'home' to her. The point is reinforced by the observation that one village – Real de Catorce in the state of San Luis Potosí – literally becomes a village of the dead in early November. The graveyard in that village has not been used in a long time and so few of the living have dead ancestors there. Almost everyone from Real de Catorce travel to their 'homes,' neighboring villages where their dead are buried to celebrate the Day of the Dead. Only the long dead remain behind to protect the village.[2]

Even those who now live far away return home for the Day of the Dead regardless of the hardship this might generate. On a commercial farm in San Diego County, California, a manager who hires a large number of migrant workers from Oaxaca had to deal with this yearly. "One day I'd have thirty or thirty-five workers in the field; the next day they'd all be gone. I'd want to fire them all but then I'd have to train new guys every year. Finally, I just shut the operation down for two weeks in order to keep my best people." Incidentally, the same manager noted that all of his workers were willing to work straight through the Christmas season and Easter week providing they could get home for the Day of the Dead.

Around the middle of October, families go to the cemeteries to invite their deceased relatives to the celebration. Some prepare formal invitations, but most of the time the announcement is informal, delivered as part of a regular visit to the cemetery. This invitation marks the beginning of the 'season' and preparations start in earnest. To outsiders, it seems like the village people have taken leave of their senses, preparing a party when the invited partygoers are all dead. As we will see later, being dead is no big deal for a Oaxaqueñan. First, let us look at that party we call the Day of the Dead.

Imagine that you are expecting some relatives or friends who live far away and can only visit on rare occasions. They are coming home to visit but circumstances prevent them from staying more than a day or two. You would pull out all the stops.

2. Martínez 1997.

A traditional Day of the Dead ofrenda in the home of Carlos, a baker in the city of Oaxaca.

You would want to make sure that their visit was the best one possible. Nothing can be allowed to interfere with it and you will do everything you can to insure a happy, harmonious reunion. Among the first things you would do is notify all of the local relatives and friends of the impending visit. You will arrange for all the locals to meet at a specific time and place, but of course you will schedule some quality time for the visitors and their closest relatives and friends. You will then plan to open up the gathering to everyone. Perhaps you would even move the gathering to a public place like a hall or hold it outdoors in some communal area such as a park.

Traditional foods such as pan de muertos (bread for the dead), tamales, and hot chocolate were placed side by side with more modern elements such as beer, Pepsi-cola, and cigarettes on this ofrenda in Zaachila.

To make sure the visitors have a good time, you will go to the store and get all of their favorite foods, favorite drinks, favorite treats, and favorite music. You would plan to have whatever meals your family traditionally has when there is a special occasion. You will use your 'good' dishes and possibly go so far as to decorate your house in a festive manner. There is no doubt you will do all you can to signal to your guests that they are special to you. You will politely refuse offers of assistance that the locals offer. You want to do it all yourself but, in the back of your mind, you know that the local folks will show up bringing potluck dishes, drinks, and other special treats or gifts. They too want to show the visitors how much they care.

On the day your guests arrive, all regular activities stop. Normal routines are discarded to be replaced by festivities. The food and the drinks will be put out and replenished constantly. With favorite music as background, the members of the family and

A close up of the ofrenda in the house of Jesus in Teotitlan del Valle. In the center of the picture is a stack of crisp tortillas (called totopos), some salt and some pan de muertos.

close friends gather in your home to visit, to gossip, to enjoy the company of the visitors and of each other. There will be a constant stream of relatives and others coming and going. The chatter is nonstop and will continue throughout the day and into the night as well. You can always catch up on lost sleep once your guests have gone.

The next day, the party might move to a larger venue where everyone, even those who know the visitors only slightly, can visit with your guests. To make this day as special as the one before, you might add some fireworks, perhaps hire a local band in addition to keeping the food and refreshments flowing. Of course, the short visit is over all too soon and your guests depart. You are sad to see them go but you are happy that you had that time with them. You sit back, reflect on the visit, enjoying those parts that went well and planning to improve on those that did not go so well.

A simple rural ofrenda from the home of Doris in Ejutla de Crespo. All of the materials on this ofrenda were purchased locally.

The people of Oaxaca in southern Mexico do exactly what you would have done in this situation. There are only slight differences between your behavior and that of the Oaxaqueñans. The visitors who live far away and come visiting for a short time happen to be dead and all the dead are coming home at once. People have to juggle their time to give their own relatives adequate time, but also to fit in visits with all of the other visitors around the village that you would like to see. This visit and the often frantic activity that comes with it combine to become what is known as *el diá de muertos.*

2. Oaxaca and Its People

The state of Oaxaca is both culturally and environmentally diverse with ecozones ranging from swampy lowlands to highland areas deeply incised by canyons and arroyos. There are roughly sixteen indigenous groups scattered across the state, each with its own language and set of customs. However, the central valleys are part of a single ecosystem and are dominated by a single indigenous group, the Zapotec. The name "Zapotec" comes from the *Náhuatl* word *Tzapotecatl* that means "the village of zapote" and refers to the large number of zapote fruit trees growing in the Oaxaca area. The Spanish corrupted the *Náhuatl* word to the present Zapotec. Of course, the locals do not call themselves Zapotec but instead are the *ben 'zaa* (the people of the clouds) or simply *'zaa* (the people).

The central valleys of Oaxaca are bordered on all sides by the Sierra Madre Mountains and share, with some local microvariations, a single ecosystem that ranges in altitude from 1150 to 1850 meters (3773 to 6070 feet) above sea level. The climate ranges from temperate to hot and from dry to humid, with the major climatic factor being rain. Some areas get rain all year while much of the valley system gets rain only during the summer months, with some regions getting very little rain at any time of the year. Generally, the center regions of each valley arm

The ruins of Monte Alban, an ancient city on top of a hill high above the city of Oaxaca (photo by Ellie Braun-Haley).

falls into the temperate zone with sufficient seasonal rainfall while the higher edges of the valleys tend to be hotter and drier.[3] Vegetation tends to be savanna-like on the valley floors.

There are three valleys in the Central Valley System: (1) an arm running west from the city of Oaxaca (containing the District of Etla); (2) another arm running east from the city (the District of Tlacolula); and (3) the longest valley running south from the city and including the districts of Zimitlán, Ocotlán, Ejutla and Mihuatlán. Since the city of Oaxaca sits where all three valleys converge, it has its own district (Cen-

---

3. Alvarez 1994: 106-107.

tro) and is considered a fourth part of the Central Valley System. According to the 1990 Census, the Central Valleys contained 797,261 people or 26.4% of the total population of the State of Oaxaca (but in area, the valleys represent only 12.6% of the total area of the state). Because the Central Valley System is geographically separable from the rest of the state, and is home to a single (but not necessarily homogeneous) ethnic/linguistic group–the Zapotec–it is possible to look at that single ethnic group and how its members celebrate the Day of the Dead.

The city of Oaxaca de Juárez has among its population representatives of all of the ethnic groups present in the state. It also has a sizeable population that considers Spanish to be its mother tongue and whose members identify with the city rather than with any ethnic home region. This group and its urban affiliations allowed data to be collected on the effects of urbanization on what is essentially a rural celebration.

A campesino traveling home with his herd to San Lorenzo a few miles west of the city of Oaxaca (photo by Ellie Braun-Haley).

Ethnicity, Variation and Loyalty

Many villagers in Oaxaca assign their loyalties to their villages rather than the poorly perceived nation of Mexico. "The Zapotec peasant has traditionally thought of himself first and foremost as a citizen of his own community. De la Fuente notes that Oaxacan villages have come to resemble small sovereign states"[4]

4. Dennis 1987: 4-5; also see De la Fuente 1965: 31-32; Kearney 1972; Newbold Chiñas 1992.

Although the typical Mesoamerican community is related to larger social entities through numerous national and religious institutions, such as governmental offices, markets ..., and patterns of religious pilgrimage, the townspeople cultivate an intense identification with their local group. Most marriages are contracted within the community, and individuals who live in a town other than the one to which their immediate family is felt traditionally to belong are considered to be outsiders.[5]

A father and his daughter rest during Day of the Dead preparations in the cemetery of San Lorenzo Cacaotepec (photo by Lissa Jones).

5. Leslie 1981: 3-4.

Women from outlying villages come to the Central de Abastos (Oaxaca's main market) on Saturday to sell their produce, flowers, or other items (photo by Lissa Jones).

This is apparent even today. Residents of one village frequently denigrate residents of neighboring villages and even many of the people living in the city of Oaxaca are quick to identify their home village within the first few minutes of meeting a stranger. Neighboring villages often speak mutually unintelligible dialects, have distinctly different traditional costumes, and have unique customs and rituals. Further, as Dennis[6] points out, neighboring communities are frequently in conflict with one another, usually over land. This situation has likely existed for many centuries.[7]

In the literature, the term "Zapotec" is often used to describe all of the indigenes in the state of Oaxaca who speak one of the Zapotec languages. However, as the intervillage rivalry and the variety of languages spoken indicate, the Zapotec people were not and are not a culturally unified collective that can be discussed the same way as the Mexica (Aztec) can. Rather, the Zapotec is a set of culturally diverse, autonomous political, social and religious units.[8] They do not see themselves as Zapotec nor do they identify with a collective beyond the village level.

This diversity makes it difficult to discuss broad concepts such as 'Zapotec religion' in the sense of religious beliefs and practices that are shared by all those Oaxaqueñans who speak some form of Zapotec. One could expect some pan–

6. Dennis 1987.

7. Spicer 1966: 82.

8. Dennis 1987: 22; also see Whitecotton 1977:271.

Mesoamerican concepts to exist just as broad Catholic concepts are common to all villages. However, each village has adopted the prehispanic beliefs and the Catholic beliefs to suit their own situations. Unlike the Mexica who had a strong central religious and civil authority enabling a consistency of religious beliefs across all Mexica villages,[9] the Zapotec lack the central authority and the consistency.

We see examples of the diversity of beliefs (both prehispanic and Catholic) in the celebration of the Day of the Dead. For example, the Catholic foundation dictates the time of year the Day of the Dead

Traditional dress from the Isthmus area. These girls took part in a celebration held in the Santo Domingo church.

Dancers from the southern valley. Wearing traditional costumes, these young women traveled to the city of Oaxaca to participate in the Guelaguetza, an annual folkdance festival.

will be celebrated but local village beliefs define the precise dates and duration of the celebration. In Xoxocotlán, the cemetery celebration occurs on October 30 at dusk while in San Dionicio, it begins in the predawn hours of November second. In Ejutla, it begins around nine a.m. and in San Felipe, the party starts at sunset. The villagers in San Antonino begin their fiesta on November third. It is not possible then to directly compare the Catholic beliefs with the prehispanic Zapotec beliefs as the latter did not exist as a collective set and the former exhibits considerable local diversity.

9. See Furst 1995 for some excellent examples.

A farmer loading animal feed onto his cart near the town of Reyes Etla.

The Family

Despite this diversity, there seems to be a dominant family type in the villages—the 'extended' or 'multigenerational' family. Several generations of one family will share the same compound or the same house. Grandparents, parents, and children are part of a single household that operates as a unified social and economic unit. Most often, sons (and their wives and children) will live in their parents' house, farming the same land as their parents, grandparents, and great-grandparents had. This creates a sense of continuity because the family as a unit will always exist even though individual members will die.

Mitla, a town east of Oaxaca de Juárez, has been continuously occupied for at least 1500 years. Julio, the patriarch of his Mitla clan, is in his eighties and shares his half-acre compound with his three sons (one deceased) and their wives. There are twelve grandchildren, eight of them married men with wives, and about fifteen great-grandchildren. His house is always crowded with at least twenty people at any one meal. Julio is happiest during these meal times because, as he says, he can look at his family and know he has done his part to keep the family growing. "There are thirty of us living here, more or less." He says with a wink. "I am never sure how many. Sometimes I think that one of my great-grandchildren could sneak a friend into the house and we'd never notice."

A family laughs together at a joke during a quiet moment in the main market in Oaxaca.

The extended family of Salvador Gonzales in Teotitlan del Valle. Salvador is a weaver by day and a guitarron player in a mariachi band at night.

He and his family have been on the same land for as long as anyone can remember. "My grandfather told me that his grandfather told him that his grandfather told him that we'd lived here for a long time before he was born. My family was here before the Spanish came." The continuity provided by an extended family provides its members with a sense of belonging and a strong sense of place. It also provides safety and comfort. Children can go to any adult for anything from solace to lunch. They can fall asleep anywhere within the family's compound in total safety and security. It is not unusual to see several young cousins sleeping together in one house one night and a different one the next.

When there is a job to do, there are many hands to help because everything benefits everyone. The men tend the fields collectively while the women as a group prepare the meals and keep an eye on the children. Building a new house or barn in a corner of the compound is quick and easy. If, for some reason, a woman needs to go to the market, she can always find someone to accompany her and another to watch the children. Of course, since there is constant interaction at all levels, there is little privacy for the individuals. Parents share their bedroom with the children. No matter where you go within the compound, others are already there before you. This can be difficult at times but people adapt. For example, young adults will go into the village to visit their friends. The parks are often crowded with young couples enjoying a few moments without any family nearby. It is interesting that these young people will not bring a girlfriend or boyfriend home to meet his or her family until the couple is considering marriage. Chances are, however, that the parents already

The family of Crisanta Lopez de Matais gathers in front of their ofrenda in the city of Oaxaca.

know of the relationship and if in favor of it, will find ways to help the youngster in his or her attempts to get out of the compound to see his or her lover. Naturally, if they are against the relationship, they will make escape very difficult, always finding things that must be done right now at home. In small communities, there can be few

Estela and Martha. The older generations are responsible for providing advice to the younger ones.

secrets and the parents know the boy or girl the son or daughter is dating. In many cases, that individual will be a distant relative or the child of a friend.

This lack of privacy for individual members is only one indication that individuals are unimportant in the grand scheme of things. Another is that few individuals will even consider making a decision without lengthy discussion with other members of the family. One young man let it be known that he would like to leave Zimitlán and go to Oaxaca de Juárez to go to university. He discussed it with his parents, one of his uncles, and his grandfather before abandoning the idea in favor of becoming a partner in his uncle's construction business. His uncle, Juan, explained what had happened.

> I talked to Carlito's father and grandfather. I also talked to my children who are closer to Carlito than any of the adults. It seems the boy did not really want to go to the city but he did not like farming, his father's occupation.

The adults listened to the boy's plans and then steered him towards a career that would keep him close to his family. Everyone knew that a move to the city would have been hard on Carlito and on everyone else. They needed to keep the family together and so they found a way. Carlito told me in private that he really wanted to become a doctor, a career that would have taken him to Oaxaca de Juárez and eventually Mexico City. He also knew that such a move would have broken his mother's heart and so backed down and stayed home.

Individuals have little privacy, independence, or freedom but they do not want these things. Katrina, a young mother of two children, could not imag-

The poorest of the poor, these children and their families live and beg on the city streets.

The wife and daughters of Salvador Gonzalez stand in the doorway to their kitchen in Teotitlan del Valle. Traditionally, the women are responsible for most of the household chores (photo by Monica Smith).

ine why anyone would want to be alone. "Who would you talk to? Who would go to the market with you?"

Sons stay in their natal home and their wives leave their homes to join their husband's family. This does not in any way reduce the contact between the new bride and her family, as most people will marry someone who is already living in the same *barrio* or neighborhood. Only the most daring would dare to court someone from another part of the village. Fewer than one in a hundred will marry someone from outside the village. New brides usually visit their mothers and their sisters daily and are constantly running into their relatives in the *barrio* and in the village.

Of course, marriage is only one stage in a person's life. I had Estela tell me about life in a village and she divided a lifespan into four major phases:

First, you are a child. During this time, you have few worries and there are lots of people there to look after you. Then you grow up and become an adult with children of your own. This is a time of great responsibility. You have the children to

look after and you have the *viejitos,* the old ones—your parents or grandparents who are too old to look after themselves. If enough time passes and misfortune hasn't taken you away, you become one of the old ones. You have few responsibilities but many of the younger ones will come to you for advice and assistance. You must do your best for them, based on your life's experiences. Finally, you die and become an ancestor. This is the least stressful stage in one's lifetime but you are not free of your obligations to the family yet. For several generations, you may be called upon for advice. You must give it freely lest someone think you have abandoned your family.

I have noticed that many families who move to the city will try to maintain the extended family structure. Large blocks of land for family compounds are prohibitively expensive so adjustments must be made. For example, the Vásquez family, originally from San Dionicio, lives in single-family homes but all are located close to one another. Of the sixteen homes on both sides of a single block of a suburban street, seven belong to and are occupied by members of the Vásquez family. The children are encouraged to socialize with their cousins and so follow the rural pattern of eating and sleeping. On a regular basis, the families congregate at the patriarch's house for meals and/or socializing. No one ever eats alone and only rarely is anyone left alone for any significant period of time.

Compadres and Comadres

The family provides an individual with most of his or her social network but there is another category of person who also becomes important in that social network.

Women of approximately the same age go through the same stages in life together. Some of them form comadre relationships, closer than those of siblings.

Man riding mule cart near San Isidro Etla. Usually the men work their own fields alone or with male kin of different generations (grandfathers, fathers, sons, and grandsons).

They are referred to as '*compadres*' or '*comadres.*' These are people who accept certain social obligations in your life and the lives of your children and who place the same obligations on you. I have seen these relationships equated to the American god-parents although, in Mexico, the arrangement is much more complicated. It is a reciprocal agreement to care for you and yours if the family is unable to do so for any reason. That is similar to the godparent but, in America, the role is passive. Among the Oaxaqueñans, the role is active with the *compadre* or *comadre* becoming part of the family much of the time. With the title of aunt or uncle, he or she dispenses advice, gifts, scoldings, and anything else an aunt or uncle would provide.

Estela, whose family owned a store, and Debora, whose family owned a restaurant, became each other's *comadres* when they were first married. Both are now in their late sixties and, over the years, have become closer than sisters. Both have been widowed and both are now the senior matriarchs in their respective families. They know each other well enough to finish each other's sentences and speak to one another in a kind of verbal shorthand intelligible only to them.

Debora told me that the relationship she has with Estela is very important. She says she has someone in Estela who knows everything about her family, even its deepest, darkest secrets, but does not have the complex set of obligations to that family that its members have. Estela's advice on a family matter will be more objective, more open than a family member's would be, as she does not have to consider the familial obligations in her advice.

Woodcarvers working at a factory in Arrazola. Most men must have two or three jobs to try to make ends meet.

Poverty, Subsistence, and Fatalism

Oaxaca is one of the poorest states in the Republic of Mexico. This poverty is most easily seen in the capital city, Oaxaca de Juárez, where beggars are on every street corner and dozens of children dressed in rags sell gum or shoe shines to the tourists. However, the villages and towns are not immune to poverty's debilitating effects. Indeed, it is the grinding poverty of the *campesinos* (peasants) that drives many of them to the city.

Margarita shares a one-room house with her husband and her widowed sister, plus her two children and her sister's four children (all of the children are under the age of seven). The only furniture they own is a single wooden bed and three plain wooden chairs. To say that they are poor is an understatement. Carlos, Margarita's

A campesino cuts and piles corn before loading it onto his cart. Much of the food these farmers eat, they grow themselves. Often, they will sell the surplus they produce in order to buy those goods they cannot grow.

husband, farms a small plot that he rents from an absentee landlord. On that plot, he grows corn and some vegetables that the family will eat rather than sell. Margarita sells peanuts in the market six days a week, but wishes that her husband could find a way to grow some food for sale as well because, on a good day, she will earn no more than thirty pesos. Her sister looks after the children and tries to gather wild plants for sale in the market, but she does not have much time for this and so rarely makes more than 10 pesos a day. By combining the sisters' incomes, this family of nine people earns just 860 pesos a month. That amounts to about 10,200 pesos per year (under $1300.00US).

Margarita's family is typical of many villagers struggling to make ends meet. But despite the problems that stem from being poor, many people are happy, or at least content. They laugh and joke about how things are going. Interestingly, they rarely discuss the future. As Carlos put it, "today is what is important. We have enough to eat. The children are all well. Life is good." When pressed about the future, he shook his head sadly. "It does not matter. It is not good to think too much about tomorrow. If I think about tomorrow, I miss today and I will feel sad." Carlos admitted that whenever he thought of the future, of what lies ahead for him and his family, he gets depressed. He expects that things will get worse. He could lose his crop. One of his children could get sick. He could hurt himself and be unable to support his family. In short, he espouses a fatalism typical of the *campesinos*.

Their basic philosophy is simple. It centers on the idea that you must always try to do your best to raise your family and to support your community but your best efforts are, in the end, of no importance. There are forces out there that capriciously and without warning will turn everything you have to dust. The best you can look forward to in the future is a 'good' death—at home, in your own bed, surrounded by your family. This is not a surprising perspective given where these people live.

Oaxaca is in a region that is seismically unstable, prone to earthquakes and volcanic activity. Rainfall is erratic and, in the best years, barely enough to meet the peoples' needs. Drought is an ever-present threat but sometimes it rains too much and the result is flooding and mudslides. Oaxaca gets hit by hurricanes from the Caribbean to the east and by monsoons that sweep in from the Pacific to the west. Just when you least expect it, natural disasters strike.

Also, because of its isolation, both geographic and social, from the rest of Mexico, there is little relief provided by the government. There is no social safety net and families are expected to look after their own. Many villagers feel that all their gov-

Market day in Tlacolula. On Sundays, many of the inhabitants of the surrounding villages gather in Tlacolula to buy and sell various items but also to visit and to gossip (photo by Lissa Jones).

ernment ever does is collect taxes and create new rules and regulations designed to make the future worse. Margarita summed it up nicely: "We are here today and happy because the land lets us be. Tomorrow, or at some later time, it will withdraw its permission. We will be evicted from this life."

A woman from the town of Mitla spinning wool in preparation for the weaving of rugs using patterns taken from the archaeological site of the same name. Several families in Mitla argue that they are the direct descendents of the original inhabitants who built the first buildings in the town almost 2000 years ago.

3. Funerals and Death

The people of Oaxaca say that the dead return for a visit with their families for one day every year and so the living celebrate their return with delight. However, it quickly becomes apparent that the dead are not limited to visiting for that one day. They may return to earth whenever they wish. Maria tells of a ride on a bus several years ago. She got on and sat down beside an old woman whom she had not seen for several years. All the way to Maria's village, they chatted and gossiped about people they both knew. When Maria got off, her friend said good-bye and they went their separate ways. It had been, for Maria, a pleasant way to pass the tedious half-hour ride home. Later she discovered that the woman on the bus had died some years before. Maria does not know why the dead woman visited her but she suspects that the woman was in need of information about her family and friends.

The visits are reciprocal in that the living can also visit the dead when they want. Many villagers visit the graves of their relatives often—perhaps three or more times a week. They do so to consult with the dead, to ask advice, or simply to update the deceased on the family's status. This would be a waste of time if the souls of the dead were locked in some afterworld place and not free to be with their living relatives in the cemetery.

It is interesting to watch one corner of the Ejutla cemetery as it is carefully avoided by those who visit the cemetery but others surreptitiously seek it out. It seems that one woman in Ejutla, after her death, acquired the reputation for being a *bruja* (a witch). No one I know dared to sit directly on the grave of the *bruja* even though everyone would casually sit on any other grave in the cemetery. Her grave, according to local folklore,

A woman choosing pan de muertos for a family ofrenda in Teotitlan del Valle (photo by Lissa Jones)

has great power in the sense that if you sit nearby her grave and wish for something (either positive or negative), your wish will come true. I was told that this power was discovered after several odd occurrences in the town. Everyone knows at least one person who has had a wish granted by the dead witch. For example, a young unmarried woman who had gotten pregnant visited her grandmother's grave (quite near the *bruja*'s grave) and, while crying, wished she hadn't become pregnant. Within a day or two, she had a miscarriage. While visiting another grave nearby, two children, a brother and a sister, got into a fight. The sister, losing her temper, wished her brother harm. He tripped on the *bruja*'s grave and broke his arm. Several other similar incidents occurred and eventually the *bruja*'s reputation grew.

Today, there is a general taboo that requires that everyone avoid that grave lest the wished-for happen. Those who must go near the grave, for example, to tend or visit adjacent graves, say that they are careful to think only positive thoughts when they are there. However, in my conversations with several women in their late 20s or early 30s, all admitted to sneaking close to the grave when no one was around and wishing for their boyfriends to ask them to marry. Knowing smiles were the only responses I received when I asked if the wishing worked.

I was first alerted to this grave when Magdalena, pointing out a man passing in the street, told us that he was not allowed to go anywhere near a certain part of the cemetery. She went on to explain that he was a bad man, very bitter, who was always thinking evil, harmful thoughts. Apparently he hated just about everyone and any contact he had with the *bruja*'s grave would almost certainly result in the downfall of whomever the man was mentally cursing at the time.

The power of the dead to affect the lives of the living is not limited to the power of a single witch. I was told that parents must be careful during the Day of the Dead or while visiting a cemetery not to scold a child. It is said that the dead are peace loving and are generally opposed to this kind of behavior. The dead, in order to protect the youngster from scolding, would take him or her home with them. In other words, the child would die. In Jalapa de Díaz near the northern border of the state of Oaxaca, there is a similar taboo about scolding children. Of course, there are many stories about the dead punishing the living for not fulfilling their obligations. Most often, the stories revolve around failures to put out the proper *ofrenda* on the Day of the Dead. The apparent punishment for this neglect is almost always death.

When I asked if there were any other ways the dead can affect the living, I was often met with a look that said: "Don't you understand anything?" Debora sat me down one day and explained that the dead affect the living every day and in every way.

> They are here. They are all around us. They help us everyday. My daughter may be dead but she is still my daughter. Oh, death makes us a little bit wiser so I can ask her advice when I need it. I go to the cemetery and sit beside her grave so she and I can have a quiet conversation. There are too many interruptions anywhere else. I tell her what is going on and what I think I need to do. She tells me in here [she touched her heart] what I should do. If she were still alive, I would do the same thing except that we would talk in our kitchen instead of the cemetery and she wouldn't have the wisdom death gives you.

One of the women who helped construct an ofrenda in the Casa Hogar para Ancianos (rest home) in San Felipe del Agua (photo by Lissa Jones).

Emelia and her daughter prepare their ofrenda in Teotitlan del Valle.

I asked if her daughter's death made those conversations harder to have. (She was killed in an automobile accident in 1994.)

"Ha! When she was alive, she lived in [the city of] Oaxaca and she was always out touring. [Debora's daughter was a professional folk dancer.] Now that she is dead, now that she is home, we are closer than before. We can talk anytime we want."

Many others agreed that the dead remained part of the family and visited often. During one conversation in Estela's *tienda*, Ernesto, who had been drinking beer all afternoon, laughingly pointed out that on the Day of the Dead, all of the houses got awfully full since there are so many more dead than there are living. Esmeralda responded with a snort.

"Shut up, you drunk. You should have listened to your mother when you were a child. Then you wouldn't be drinking so much and showing your ignorance. You are a disgrace to your family."

"It was just a joke! Papa knows I was only having fun with you."

"Ha! Our friend comes all the way from Canada to learn our ways and you behave like a fool. If your father was alive, he'd soon set you straight."

"*Tia* Esmeralda, I am no fool!"

"Then tell us what you know to be true." she demanded.

With frequent glances at Esmeralda, the floor, and me, Ernesto explained that soon after death, the people are anxious to visit with their living relatives. They come often but as time passes and more people die, the dead tire of the contact with the

A couple clears weeds off a grave in the cemetery at San Lorenzo Cacaotepec. In this cemetery, most of the graves are simply mounds of dirt with a crude cross.

A relative of Jesús Hernandez Jiménez prepares to decorate the family's ofrenda.

living. By the time their grandchildren are grown and are beginning to have children of their own, the dead grandparents only come to visit on the Day of the Dead and they don't stay long—just long enough to fulfill their familial obligations. When the great-grandchildren are themselves grown, the dead grandparents don't even bother with the Day of the Dead except perhaps once in a long while. They have far too much to do in their own village. It seems that the dead visit only those living people with whom they spent a considerable time while alive. They help them and punish them if they forget their obligations but once the people they knew die, they lose interest in this world. Memories of the living and of the dead fade together.

This fits with the general attitudes the people of Oaxaca have about death. According to many people I spoke to, death is a natural phenomenon that everyone must prepare for. The ideal is to die at home in bed with as many loved ones as possible close by. Again, ideally, when death comes, it is no surprise. It comes when one is old and after there have been 'messengers' such as bouts of serious illness heralding the impending death. Even in the absence of such clues or messengers, once a person reaches a certain age, he or she begins preparations (around age 80 if one is in good health or by the mid 60s if the person is in poor health). Most of the preparations have no physical manifestation, as they are internal. The individual is preparing himself or herself both mentally and emotionally. When the death is accepted

as inevitable and impending, when the individual is, in his or her mind, ready, he or she will signal that readiness to the family by offering up such comments as: "The next time we meet, I might be dead" or "I will be in the ground soon." Family members are not surprised when such statements are made. They are saddened but not surprised. Often, conversations about deceased relatives are used to announce the senior's readiness to die: "My sister has been dead for twenty years. Soon, I will be seeing her again."

It seems that it is up to the elder to begin the process and the family's preparations. The other family members will not initiate any discussions out of respect for the elder no matter how ill that person has been or how old he or she is. As Carmen noted: "My mother is very old and very wise. She will know when death is coming. When she knows, she will tell us. Until then, we wait." When I asked her why, she responded: "If I, her

Open graves await their occupants in the Panteon Jardín on the outskirts of the city of Oaxaca.

daughter, talk about her death, she might think I want her to hurry up and be dead. I do not want that. I could not even suggest it."

Her mother, who says she is in her mid 80s (although no one is sure of her precise age), added this: "A person knows when to get ready for death. One morning, one afternoon, the soul stretches, tries to wiggle out of its body. That is the signal to begin preparation." Another elder, Carmen's mother's neighbor, disagreed with her. "The message comes not when you are awake but when you are asleep. In a dream, your soul appears tired, worn out. It is unable to carry around the body much longer."

The elderly women argued for some time about this without coming to a resolution. However, they did agree that the soul (which is apparently separate from the mind) is what signals the coming death. It attempts in some way to

Newer graves nestle between older ones in the Ejutla cemetery.

leave the body either in a dream or when the body is awake. However the message is delivered, the person begins his or her preparations in response to it. Then they, in turn, alert the rest of the family to prepare.

The individual who believes he or she is about to die seems quite relaxed about it. They know that time has no relevance in the realm of the supernatural and, although the soul is tired and ready to leave the body, it could take several years before the soul actually gets around to leaving. They also know that there will be other signs usually in the form of bouts of illness or gradual debilitation.

When an individual dies after the messages have been received and the preparations are done, the surviving family members are saddened and go through a period of grief and mourning. The funeral is a sad affair yet it is subdued. People cry but there are no 'grand gestures' of grief. This changes when someone dies suddenly without warning. Estela's son-in-law, Enrique, lost his sister in a bus accident that killed a number of people. He has yet to come to terms with her death. The death of his mother at age 78 at home in bed was far less traumatic than the death of his sister. Debora lost her daughter in another traffic accident and still feels the loss after several years. It seems that when a person 'eases' out of life, the sense of loss is much weaker than when a person is 'wrenched' or 'ripped' out of life. The latter involves a great deal of questioning and self–examination among the living.

An elaborate headstone marks the grave of a child who lived less than a week. Many children's graves will bear a statue of an angel as this one does.

Several people told me that the typical *ofrendas* built for *el Día de Muertos* are meant for those dead who have been dead for at least a year. Sometimes, the altars will include photographs or other remembrances of a specific deceased (or of more than one person) but never of a newly deceased relative. Carlos said that this year his family was only going to make a small altar because his uncle died just recently (one or two months before I spoke to him) but next year, they will be making a really big one especially for him. Traditionally, on the Day of the Dead following the first anniversary of the death of a family member, the family will construct a special altar especially for that loved one in addition to the regular one. This *nueva ofrenda* will probably include a photograph of the family member and consist of all of the favorite things of that one person to welcome him or her home the first time. The altar (minus the food) will occasionally be left up for the full year and not be dismantled until after the subsequent Day of the Dead celebration.

When asked the reason for the delay of a year before welcoming the newly deceased into the family home, the responses were varied but all related to the afterlife rather than this life. For example, I was told that the soul of the newly dead was not allowed to leave wherever they were residing for the first little while. Debora suggested that the soul was not used to heaven and if it were allowed to come home too soon, it would be sad and try to remain on earth somehow (perhaps as a wandering spirit or ghost). So the deceased had to remain in the afterlife to get used to the idea that it was dead before being allowed to visit their old home. Estela modified this idea and simply said that the newly deceased, being the new kid on the block, had to remain behind and look after things while the older hands (those who had been deceased at least a year) went off to the celebration.

I would have thought that the families would be anxious to welcome the newly deceased home soon after the death and the funeral as that is when the emotional attachment to these people is at its greatest. However, the tradition of the *nueva ofrenda* insures that at least a year has passed before the family and the deceased come together again.

I can see two reasons for delaying this confrontation. One is emotional while the other is pragmatic. The emotional one suggests that after the passing of a year, the family has completed the first stages of grief and have begun to come to terms with the death of the loved one. By waiting a year for the welcoming home of the deceased, the family is better able to happily welcome their dead. The time for sadness has passed. As many of my informants told me, "The morning of November first is a sad time. We cry but by noon, the tears are all used up and we are happy again. Our dead want us to be happy." On the other hand, in prehispanic times, the dead were disinterred and invited physically to attend the celebration. The skulls of the deceased were cleansed, painted, named and celebrated with. If the newly dead were invited too and attended the very first Day of the Dead after their death, their bodies could be still very much in evidence. The body of an individual who, for example, has been dead for only two months would have only begun to decay. To disinter him and invite him to the celebration physically would be a disgusting affair. However, by waiting a minimum of a year before inviting the deceased to the celebration and therefore giving the body sufficient time to decompose down to a skeleton, that possibility is eliminated.

Several villagers described the place where one goes when one dies. It is, according to them, not much different from the villages of the living. Located in some vague spot to the south, this place, the Village of the Dead, has all the elements of an earthly village and the dead pursue their former occupations. However, there are some significant differences. There are never shortages of food. No babies can be born into the Village of the Dead. There are no earthquakes, hurricanes, or revolutions. In short, it is a paradise where the dead have enough of all the good things and none of the bad. In addition, day and night are reversed. When the sun sets in the land of the living, it rises on the land of the dead. This is why, as the Oaxaqueñans say, the dead can move around so easily at night. It is day for them.

The people who have the clearest picture of the Village of the Dead are the elderly, who, in their own minds, will soon be occupying a house there. The younger folks are too busy living to give it much thought and will avoid discussing it whenever possible.

Funerals in the Oaxacan villages are simple affairs. They are hastily arranged and take place as soon as the deceased's friends and relatives from the surrounding area can get there. If the deceased was elderly, the gathering is a subdued and relaxed farewell. Funerals of young people are more emotional (as the death was usually unanticipated). In either case, all who knew the deceased would make an effort to attend. The one exception is the funeral of an infant or toddler. These are usually private affairs with only the parents, grandparents, and siblings in attendance.

In Ejutla de Crespo, there is a funeral home that could perhaps serve as a metaphor for the Oaxacan attitudes towards death and life. This funeral home is tiny, with barely enough room for the coffins that hug three of its bright blue walls. These coffins are piled three high and on top of one such pile sat a set of huge speakers out of which the latest Mexican popular music blared. It is as if the funeral home was signaling that life and death are one in the same.

Simple graves in Ejutla de Crespo. Many, like these, are treated as mini-gardens.

Maria with her daughter in the market in Etla. In a few years, the daughter will begin to help her mother in the market and at home.

These women in Tlacolula gather what they need for the Day of the Dead.

In Etla, as in many of the villages, the market is the exclusive domain of the women. Men are sometimes recruited to carry the heavy purchases.

A woman transports flowers from the market to the cemetery in Xoxocotlán.

People gathering in the cemetery of San Lorenzo Cacaotepec. The early crowds are mostly women as the men are still at work.

On the Day of the Dead, flowers seem to be everywhere in the markets as in this market in Ejutla.

The Day of the Dead market in the city of Oaxaca is for both locals and tourists. Tourists can buy all kinds of souvenirs of the Day of the Dead such as mini-coffins, tiny gravestones, and skeletal figurines.

4. The Day of the Dead Markets

The markets in the central valley of Oaxaca normally follow the Mexican pattern. Each town and village has one day set aside as the Market Day and, on that day, buyers and sellers gather to do business. The area overflows with permanent and temporary stalls as well as *ambulantes* (individuals who wander through the crowds selling their wares from carts, boxes, or bags). On the other days of the week, only a small number of permanent stalls in the market area are open.

As the Day of the Dead approaches, a change takes place. Beginning about a week before the Day of the Dead, more and more temporary outdoor stalls appear and remain open for the remainder of the week. Some sell items used in the preparation phase of the celebration. Others, taking advantage of the increased trade, set up their stalls to sell everything from denim jeans and cotton aprons to pots and pans, dishes and fireworks. As the week progresses, markets grow until on October

A fruit and vegetable vendor in the market in Etla.

31 they reach their maximum size. The one exception occurs in Mihuatlán at the extreme southern end of the Oaxaca Valley. There, they hold a gigantic Day of the Dead Market that begins around 7:00 P.M. on October 30 and ends early in the morning of the following day. The markets on the subsequent days, unlike in the other villages, are significantly smaller than this all-night market.

The actual number of booths devoted exclusively to Day of the Dead items is quite small in Ejutla and in Ocotlán and they are scattered in an apparently random manner throughout the market area. In fact, many of the regular vendors simply add a few Day of the Dead items to their regular inventories. The same vendors modify their inventories in the same way every year for this market so

A woman selling nísperos (a small fruit similar to a kumquat) at the market in Ejutla.

that those who live in the villages know exactly where to get everything they need without searching.

This pattern of increased activity in the markets and the addition of special holiday items to regular inventories can also be seen in the small local markets within the city of Oaxaca (for example, at the El Merced, Porfirio Díaz and Benito Juárez markets). However, at the Central de Abastos, the main market that services all of the city of Oaxaca, there is a significant variation in the pattern. There is, as in the villages, an increase of activity and the introduction of special items, but there, they have a special area set aside for this activity. At the Central de Abastos, a normally vacant outdoor area adjacent to the meat market becomes filled with a special Day of the Dead Market. Row after row of stalls spring up ten days before the holiday.

This Day of the Dead Market is a dynamic place that changes its character daily. For example, in 1997, as the market employees were setting up the stalls, vendors moved into them. Sometimes, it was the rightful seller who had paid a small fee for that specific location (some occupying the exact same space year after year) but more often than not, it was a squatter who moved in, a vendor who had not paid a fee but who was not going to miss an opportunity to sell his wares from this prime location for the day. On subsequent days, the first vendors to arrive in the morning grabbed the choice spots regardless of who had occupied them the previous day. Each booth would then, by the end of the market season, have housed a series of vendors until the rightful occupant arrived to claim his location. It was not until October 31 that a reasonable measure of stability was achieved. By then, everyone who had paid the fee had occupied their designated locations and all of the vendors who sold the perishable items had also arrived.

In 1997, as in previous years, the market was fairly large with 284 booths arranged in four rows. There were also ambulatory vendors with pushcarts or arm-fuls of products ranging from Day of the Dead items such as ceramic skeletal figures and *veladoras* (candles in glass containers) to everyday items such as fresh garlic and children's underwear.

In the Central de Abastos Day of the Dead Market, one can find all of the tradi-tional materials readily available in vast quantities. For example, thirty-three stalls were devoted to the flowers of the dead (*flores de muertos*) and another fifty-four sold fruit. Two dozen booths sold bread for the dead (*pan de muertos*). In addition, unlike the village markets, booths selling similar items tended to be clustered together. Eighteen of the twenty-four *pan de muertos* stalls formed a single, almost continuous line. The fruit vendors occupied most of the western wall of the market and the flower vendors clustered at the northern end.

While many of the booths sold traditional items, all of which could be found in the village markets as well, many others sold items that could only be purchased at the Central de Abastos. These included skeletal figurines made of clay, rope, wire, paper or plastic. These figurines, often humorously depicting specific occupations, are a popular tourist item although many locals buy them too.

In the city of Oaxaca as in other parts of the valley, these markets are, without question, one of the highlights of the year. Several businesses do a significant per-centage of their sales during this time period. Indeed, some villages specialize in Day of the Dead items and rely on this market for survival. San Antonino grows the marigolds and cockscomb sold in the few days before the celebration and Ejutla manufacturers make the liquor-filled and *calabaza* paste candies sold throughout the valley. Many families across the region grow a few extra jicamas or oranges or spend their spare time constructing skeletal figures for sale during this time. Whatever the social or religious benefit derived from the Day of the Dead, it is also a major eco-nomic boost for the entire region.

Day of the Dead Cottage Industries

It is difficult to determine the precise economic impact of the Day of the Dead on the Oaxaca area but there can be no doubt that the celebration brings a major infu-sion of cash into the area. It provides a considerable opportunity for locals to gain some income for two major reasons: Many Oaxaqueñans return home for the cel-ebration, often from considerable distances, and so the demand for all regularly purchased items (such as food and flowers) increases sharply. There are also a num-ber of items relating to the Day of the Dead that are made or produced locally by individuals or small family enterprises and sold for only a short time—about one month out of the year.

Pan de Muertos

Every *ofrenda* must have some *pan de muertos* on it, and every time someone is served hot chocolate, they must be given the bread of the dead to go with it. Neither would be complete without it so that during the weeks immediately before and after the Day of the Dead, there is a huge demand for this special bread. It is not unusual to see people buying *canastos* (large baskets) filled with *pan de muertos*.

Antonio, owner of a *pan de yema* (sweet bread) bakery in Santo Domingo Etla Alto, northwest of the city of Oaxaca, told us that his bakery normally operates for between ten and twelve hours a day six days a week. However, for between three weeks to a month before the Day of the Dead and a week after it, the bakers work seven days a week around the clock, stopping only when the crew is too exhausted to continue. All of their meals are brought into their place of work and consumed as they work.

Most *pan de muertos* is oval shaped with the added *cabecita* (little head) but some bakeries form the bread into different shapes. I have seen some crude animal shapes (sheep and turkey) but the majority were human-like. The loaves shaped like people are long and thin with slits to indicate the location of the arms and legs and a cabecita of the appropriate size is placed where the head should be. There is never anything fancy about these loaves and the shapes are crude and suggestive rather than detailed or realistic. In my discussions with the bakers, they could not offer any

Antonio, a baker in Santo Domingo Etla Alto adds the cabecitas to the bread for the dead.

explanation for this type of bread. Joaquim, a baker in his thirties from the barrio of Xochimilco in the city of Oaxaca, told me that his family has been baking these shapes for as long as anyone can remember for no other reason than that they have always been doing it that way.

Interestingly, when I asked about other shapes, Joaquim laughed and told how he and his wife experimented with baking a *pan de muertos* in the shape of a cross with a *cabecita* at the top of the long section. He said they made a large batch of crosses in 1989 and took them to the market along with their regular human-shaped pan de muertos. Not one cross was sold during the market. "No one wanted to buy the crosses. Some people didn't even want to look at them. I think we lost a lot of business that year."

There is another form of *pan de muertos* but it is rare and considered quite inedible. Large loaves of *pan de yema* are baked without *cabecitas* but with special shapes attached to the top surface. These are usually cut out shapes of leaves or flower petals. Once the bread has cooled, the cut out shapes are painted in bright colors (the reason the bread is inedible). The end results are large loaves covered with three-dimensional vases full of flowers or plants. They are used as decoration on the *ofrendas* or, more frequently, as centerpieces for the family's dinner table during the holiday.

In the Benito Juárez market in 1997, I noticed that at least one baker of regular white bread (*bolillos*) was trying to get involved in the Day of the Dead. She had for

Pan de muertos piled up on an ofrenda from Teotitlan del Valle. Unlike most ofrendas, this one contains a representative of the baby Jesus.

sale several buns that had been shaped to look like human long bones (much like North American dog biscuits). They were roughly twice as expensive as her regular buns but they seemed to be attracting a crowd of the curious in the market. Even if they did not sell, they certainly drew a crowd to her location increasing her sales of other breads. I spoke to her toward the end of the day when most of her bread had been sold and Juanita was preparing to go home. She and her husband have a small bread oven that her husband's father had built. They and their children get up at four in the morning to prepare the dough and bake the bread. She has two large *canastos* of fresh bread to take to the market every day while her husband goes to work and the children go to school. She stays at the market until most or all of the bread is gone. Sometimes, Juanita tells me, she is there until 6:00 or 7:00 in the evening. However, she did say that since she started making a few 'bone' *bolillos*, she has been able to go home by 3:00 in the afternoon.

Cabecitas (Muñecas)

All of the *pan de muertos* have small heads made from flour dough set into them (this is what distinguishes *pan de muertos* from regular bread). These heads are called *cabecitas* or *muñecas* (or sometimes *calaveritas* although this usually refers to "little skulls"). The *cabecitas* range in size from less than a centimeter across to as large as ten centimeters across although the most common size is between two and three centimeters. Starting very early in October, these *cabecitas* begin to appear in the market in small and medium sizes so that they can be available for those who are going to bake their own *pan de muertos*. Towards the end of the month, the larger and more fanciful of the heads appear.

According to Paulina, who lives in Ejutla, she and her family begin to make the *cabecitas* in late July or early August. The family has three ceramic molds made by her grandfather in the 1960s—a tiny saint face, an average sized Mary and an average sized Jesus. From start to finish, the process of completing a single head takes three or four days but the family can produce as many as a hundred of each size in a single batch. In August and September, the family produces one or two batches a week and in October, they spend the first three weeks producing a batch a day.

First the dough for the batch is mixed. They use wheat flour (sometimes corn flour as well) mixed with salt, a little vegetable oil and water. The mixture is kneaded into thick dough slightly heavier in consistency than the average bread dough. Small pieces of the dough are roughly shaped into a flat oval and the base is twisted or pulled to create a tail about one half to one centimeter in length. Then this oval is pushed into the mold, which adds the three dimensional face and rounds the rough edges. It is then set aside on a metal tray to dry in the sun. This process is repeated until all of the dough is used up. The next day, the heads are given a base coat of paint (usually a cheap acrylic available in one liter jars) and again set aside to dry. Later that same day or the next, the details are painted in (eyes, cheeks, lips, highlights on the headdress if any, and the like). In Paulina's family, the children, aged ten to fourteen, are the ones who apply the detail paint. The *cabecitas* are once again set aside to dry for about a week or ten days before packing them into plastic bags according to size.

Ceramic Skeletons and Skulls

These skeletal figures, ranging in size from two or three centimeters in height to as large as 20 centimeters tall are almost always hand made from clay and heavy wire. They depict skeletons engaged in everyday activities that are instantly recognizable. These activities range from selling meat to laying bricks to dentistry. They are meant to portray the specific occupations so that people can buy them for others who engage in those professions.

Cabecitas for sale in the Central de Abastos in Oaxaca.

Most of the figurines are made by local individuals and/or families and are sold on the downtown streets or in the Market of the Dead at Central de Abastos by the people who made them or in the shops catering to the tourist. Prices fluctuate widely but did follow a basic trend. The wandering vendors who sold their figures in the *zócalo* (town square) or along the *andador* (tourist walkway) had the lowest prices. At the Market of the Dead where vendors had to pay a fee for a booth and the public came specifically to buy Day of the Dead items, the prices were a third higher. However, in the stores along the *andador* or near the *zócalo*, the prices jumped significantly. The same figurines, probably made by the same people who were selling them on the street for 6 to 12 pesos or in the market for 10 to 18 pesos, were selling for between 30 and 50 pesos in the tourist

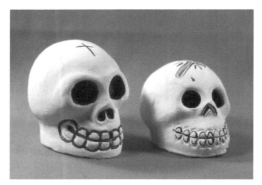

Ceramic skulls have become more common in the Day of the Dead Markets as tourist interest in the celebration has grown. Meant as tourist souvenirs, these skulls are finding their way onto local ofrendas

Ceramic figurines for sale to tourists at the day of the Dead market in the Central de Abastos.

A removable ceramic skeletal priest in a coffin.

Most of the heads used for making bread for the dead are generic human faces. Only in recent years have unusual ones, like this skeletal face, begun to appear.

A ceramic skeletal drummer. One can find nearly all occupations and pastimes represented in skeletal form.

stores. Ironically, in all three locations, the major purchaser of the figurines was the tourist. Only rarely do the locals buy them.

Ceramic skulls are, however, gaining in popularity locally. They are made by pushing clay into a mold and then removing them and letting them dry in the sun. Some manufacturers, usually individuals or families, cut crosses or other geometric shapes from the forehead or top of the head before the clay hardens. Once hard, the skulls are usually painted white with highlights of various colors added. The geometric holes, cut earlier, are covered in clear colored plastic to permit light to come through. They are more popular with the locals than the figurines and they are often seen as part of the Day of the Dead decorations in homes in the city of Oaxaca.

Ceramic Vessels

The Day of the Dead is a time when some families purchase new pots for cooking the *mole negro* and new *comales* for cooking the tortillas. It is also a time when incense burners are needed. The makers of incense burners produce them in small numbers for sale as an extra source of income in October. Leticia, a farmer's wife in Ocotlán, makes about fifty of them in her spare time in July, August, and September. She sells them only on Fridays in the month of October and usually sells out by the week before the Day of the Dead. They are three-legged bowls (about 10 cm across) to which she adds little hand formed figures such as skeletons or angels on the rims. These items sold extremely well to tourists. She laughs at one tourist couple who gladly paid thirty pesos for one of those burners in 1997. She cannot believe that they would pay that much but if they are, she is willing to invest more time and

A three-legged incense burner used only for the Day of the Dead.

energy producing them. She invited me to visit her home in 1998, saying that the Day of the Dead celebration in her home was going to be the best ever if the tourists come back then.

Paper Products

There are many Day of the Dead products that are made from paper. The most famous is the *papel picado*, sheets of tissue paper with designs cut out of them using sharp chisel-like punches. A few families purchase them every year but since they are all made elsewhere by specialists and imported into the Oaxaca area for the celebration, they are very expensive (as much as 20 to 40 pesos per sheet). Another imported paper item is a board game with a death theme. Similar to Snakes and Ladders, it features skeletons and graves and is meant to amuse the children who will be spending the night at the cemetery with their parents on November 2. The games are simply large sheets of thin cardboard printed in color on one side but require a large printing press for their production.

The rest of the paper products are made locally, always by individuals or families rather than by businesses. They include (a) paper skeleton puppets, (b) sets of pallbearers, and (c) miniature replicas of tombs. These products are often made with recycled materials such as cigarette packets and match boxes and so do not require much capital outlay. One family in Oaxaca specializes in the making of miniature tomb replicas and can produce several hundred of the objects in a few weeks but they will begin collecting the materials immediately after the celebration for the following one. Alejandro, a nineteen year old, has been making the tombs for five or six years and is quite proud of his work. His miniatures each consist of a matchbox

Puppet skeletons found at the Day of the Dead market in Etla. They are made to amuse the children in the cemeteries on November 2nd.

Children playing with the puppet skeletons in the cemetery in Xoxocotlán.

glued on top of a cigarette pack with a small cross of twigs or sticks added. The whole thing is then painted a deep blue and edged with white paint.

There are a few people using papier mache (in Mexico, the paper is soaked and mashed into a pulp rather than used in strips) to make skulls and masks that are light-weight. One or two families make these items but they are almost exclusively for the tourist market and so do not have much of an impact on the Day of the Dead on Oaxaca itself.

Incense

Copal, a tree sap that once dried is used as incense, comes in two grades –the lower grade which is gray, cloudy and has a number of inclusions, mostly bits of tree bark, and the higher grade which is clear and tends to be amber yellow. Both types are available much of the year but as the Day of the Dead approaches, there are more vendors selling copal. It is imported from the mountains to the south and west where it is collected in the wild. Because it is gathered in the wild and has to travel a fair distance to market, it is an expensive commodity. Twenty grams of the low grade copal sells for ten pesos while the high quality stuff can cost up to twice that. Because of the price, the locals buy the low grade incense in small quantities wrapped in newspaper packets. Some of the more wealthy residents of the city of Oaxaca would buy fairly large quantities of the high quality copal. However, the residents of Ejutla laugh at this waste of money. The coarser material generates a great deal of smoke while the high grade stuff smells sweeter but is much cleaner burning. The people from Ejutla think that the smoke is more important than the smell, so the cheaper kind is better. They think the city people are just showing off and making fools of themselves doing it.

Chocolate, Spices, and Other Foodstuffs

Chocolate–Hot chocolate is a favorite social drink offered every time someone comes to visit, and since, during the Day of the Dead, more people than usual are visiting, the demand for chocolate increases. The major beneficiaries of this increased demand are the commercial chocolate factories who stockpile chocolate beginning in August of each year. The chocolate, grown on the Pacific coast

Isaac Vasquez carries an incense burner of copal to his ofrenda in Teotitlan del Valle. In that village, incense can only be placed in front of the ofrenda after 3:00 PM on November 1st.

of Oaxaca is brought to the city of Oaxaca in the form of raw beans, is sold directly to the factories where sugar, water, cinnamon and other ingredients are added to roasted and ground chocolate to create a thick paste. This paste is formed into balls, sticks or cakes or reground into powdered chocolate. The processed chocolate is then sold from the factory outlets adjacent to the 20 de Noviembre market downtown.

Spices–Several different types of chiles (hot peppers) are used to make *mole negro* (a traditional sauce) and other spices such as cinnamon, cloves, and the like are used for the stewed or candied fruit dishes. The growing of the peppers is a specialized, large-scale operation requiring specialized equipment for drying and roasting. Because of these requirements, only a few farmers specialize in these crops. Everyone relies on the chile farmers for their dried spices used in the preparations for the Day of the Dead.

Leaves and Husks–Tamales of two kinds are served during the Day of the Dead. Both are available commercially but most families make their own. One, a tamal with a filling of chicken, *mole negro* and *masa* (corn dough) is wrapped in a banana leaf while the other, a sweet tamal filled with *masa* and bits of fruit (usually pineapple) is put inside a corn husk. The need for banana leaves created a source of income for women living at the south end of the Oaxaca Valley. There some banana trees are

Detail of an ofrenda from Teotitlan del Valle. This one is traditional with a number of prepared foods such as black beans and hot chocolate on it.

Tamales consisting of chicken, mole negro, and corn dough wrapped in a banana leaf are found on every ofrenda including this one from the city of Oaxaca.

A multi-level ofrenda from Teotitlan del Valle that is ready for the dead. It is a feast for several senses including taste, sight, and smell.

grown (and others are wild). They harvest about 30 percent of the leaves from each tree and then slit each leaf down the center, removing the central shaft. By doing this, the women acquire about six tamal wraps from each leaf at no cost other than their own labor. The leaf wraps are then sold at the village markets. The cornhusks are byproducts of corn farming and must be gathered when the corn is green. They require about two to three weeks to dry in the sun and so need a special rack or space where they can be dried without interference. Any family that is growing corn can produce them although only a few women in Ejutla bother with it, as most of the market customers are farmers. However, those who do get involved in preparing the corn husk tamal wraps can sell them for ten centavos each. Juanita, whose husband and brother-in-law share a small field, earns between 200 and 250 pesos for her efforts. She uses all of the money on her *ofrenda* saying that the corn husks allow her to get some new dishes or a new table cloth each year, a luxury she admits that she could not afford otherwise.

Panela–At this time of year, many families will make special treats such as candied fruit or *ponché*, a hot, cider-like drink. In addition to the fruit, the main ingredient is *panela*, a coarse brown cane sugar. This is commercially produced on large plantations but there are also several families that grow small amounts of sugar cane and produce *panela* for sale at the Day of the Dead markets.

Mole and Other Prepared Foods

Most families prefer to make their own candied fruit, particularly stewed *manzanitas* (a crabapple like fruit), candied *calabaza* and *ponché*. However, there are always some people who lack the time, energy, or talent to do so. That opens up a small market for those who make more than their family needs and so can offer some for sale. There was only one booth in the Ejutla market that offered these items for sale as most of it is offered by word of mouth. Estela ran short of stewed *manzanitas* one year and sent her *muchacha* to get some from a neighbor lady who had excess. Apparently everyone in the neighborhood knew that this woman had extra for sale.

Mole negro on the other hand is big business. Again, if possible, the women of the household prefer to make their own black spicy sauce but, for many, it is not possible. As a substitute, there is a mole concentrate the thickness of a heavy paste. It is generally available all year round in the same locations that sell cheese and chocolate. I found that only professionals make this sauce for sale, as it requires large pots and extended cooking time on stoves with controlled heating.

Lozaro operates a chocolate factory and *molino* (a place where corn and other foods are ground into flour) in the city of Oaxaca but also makes *mole negro*. During the off season, he only operates the *mole* factory three to four days a week (using only two or three of his vats) but for all of October, the plant operates six days a week at full capacity producing up to 200 liters of concentrate each day.

Sugar skulls and animals made using the alfeñique method. They are available in all sizes. Note the aluminum foil strip on the forehead.

Candies

Alfeñique–The white sugar candy skulls and candy animals are made using a technique called *alfeñique* that has its roots in the Arab world. "The Arabs brought the name and the technique to Spain and from there it traveled to Mexico."[10] The range of objects that can be made by this technique is theoretically limited only by the imagination of the craftsperson but in practice there are only a limited variety of items being made. These fall neatly into two major categories based on manufacturing technique: (1) Sugar Skulls–Candy skulls are made first by boiling sugar in water until the mixture begins to thicken, at which point a small amount of lemon juice is added. Some of the liquid is poured into a hollow two-piece mold (of clay, brass or wood) and spun so that the force will push the liquid against the mold as it cools. According to Mozzi,[11] this technique is referred to as *vaciado*. This is repeated a number of times until the candy reaches the desired thickness. When it is completely cooled, the mold pieces are separated and the candy removed. At that point, it is decorated using icing piping. (2) Sugar Shapes–In addition to skulls, there are a wide range of animals (such as sheep, pigs and chickens) as well as angels and other shapes such as coffins, baskets of flowers and tiny plates of food. They are all made using a mixture of beaten egg whites, powdered sugar, water and a binding agent called *chautle* that becomes a soft pliable white paste (*Chautle* is a binding agent made from the corms [pseudobulbs] of a ground orchid [*Bletia campanulata*]). Depending on the desired object being made, the paste was pressed into molds or hand shaped. If necessary, the paste could be colored with ordinary food coloring and decorated with icing sugar piping.

Anise-filled candies that are made only for the Day of the Dead. Any left over are shipped to Japan around mid-November.

Anise Filled Candies–These candies, which are hollow sugar shells filled with an anise flavored liquor, are available in a wide variety of shapes such as angels, harps, sheep and wreaths. The shell is made on two pieces using molds. The two halves are then glued together with a liquid sugar after the filling has been added. In Ejutla, Magdalena's family makes and sells these candies only for the Day of the Dead. The rest of the year, they run a leather working shop and store. Any excess candies they have in November are shipped to Japan where there is some demand for the sweet confection. Magdalena's family uses the income from the candy sales to supplement the income from the store.

10. Mozzi 1997: 20.
11. Mozzi 1997: 23.

Doris and Ellie buying various candies at the Day of the Dead market in the city of Oaxaca.

Calabaza Paste Candies–Two elderly sisters in Ejutla make a kind of candy using pumpkin or squash seed paste (the actual ingredient list is a closely guarded secret). These candies are colored and shaped like miniature fruits including watermelon, banana, jicama, oranges and others. Some even have a wedge cut out of them to show the inside flesh of the fruit. They are sold individually but most are packaged into small wooden boxes (about 8 by 8 centimeters in size) resembling fruit crates. They are available all year round but become particularly important during the Day of the Dead, as they are popular as gifts. Teresa, one of the sisters, bragged that certain families in the city of Oaxaca will drive all the way to Ejutla to buy their candy fruit. She said one family buys 30 boxed sets every year. Carlota, the other sister, believes that they sell more of the sets in October than they do the rest of the year but that it is getting harder and harder to keep up with the demand. She said, when they were younger (around 50, according to her), they could stay up all night for a week making the candies which are best if eaten within a week or ten days of being made. Now, Carlota argues, Teresa, who is 74, is getting too old for that and has to rest more frequently. She, on the other hand, can still handle the pace. She is only 72.

Both Teresa and Carlota are concerned that when they die, there will be no one in the family to carry on the candy making tradition. "Who will make us the candies and put them on our *ofrendas* after we die?" asks Carlota, only half seriously. Teresa responded that it didn't really matter because both of them have eaten so many of the candies that they wouldn't want any more ever. I got the sense that these sisters, who are very close, make the candies for something to do and to provide opportunities to talk with neighbors and friends. While I was there, two women came to buy candies. The transaction took only a few seconds but the women talked to the sisters for over a half hour over cups of hot chocolate. The cost of the chocolate consumed by the visitors was, in all likelihood, more than the profit made from the candies that they bought.

Chocolate Skulls–Edible chocolate skulls are found in Oaxaca but they are all made elsewhere in Mexico and imported. Unlike the local products, they are professionally boxed and labeled. In addition, they are considerably more expensive and so are not as popular with the locals. Most of the sales of these kinds of candies are to tourists and take place in the Benito Juárez Market close to the center of the city. Only a few individuals earn money from the sale of these items and then only make the retail profit since they must buy these items wholesale.

Flowers

There are three types of flowers that predominate at this time of year:

(1) Veruche, a yellow wild flower known as the *flor de muertos*, is picked by women and children and sold door-to-door or in the streets. It is not sold in any market that I know of nor do I know of anyone who grows the plant although it is an essential part of the celebration and is therefore in demand. Several of the women I spoke to in Ejutla told me they and their children spent much of the week before the Day of the Dead gathering veruche.

A farmer returns home from the market in Ejutla with his bicycle loaded down with marigolds (cempasúchitl).

Estela buys the marigolds she needs to prepare her ofrenda in Ejutla. The Mexican marigolds are much larger and taller than the North American varieties that originated in Africa.

(2) Cockscomb (*cresta de gallo* or *borla de Santa Teresa*), a tall reddish purple flower, is both commercially grown and grown by corn farmers who use the outside edges of their fields as flower plots. In San Antonino Castillo Velasco, there are a number of people who grow nothing else but cockscomb and the other *flor de muertos* – marigolds.

(3) The most common *flor de muertos*, marigolds (*cempasúchitl*), is, like cockscomb, grown on both a large and a small scale. San Antonino is well known as the village that specializes in these flowers and the people who live there are justly proud of their specialization and fiercely determined to keep hold of the monopoly they presently enjoy. Laura, who grows marigolds while her husband works as a migrant farm worker in California, clearly resents the people from other villages who plant a few marigolds for extra income. "If they want to grow some for their own *ofrenda*, I can understand that. But these people want to take food from my family's mouths.... We have been growing the *flor de muertos* for generations and they want to take that from us."

In these days of fierce competition, Laura says she has had to take some pretty serious precautions. For example, she cuts her flowers before they have been pollinated so that they will not produce any seeds. She also covers her flower beds with fine netting to keep the pollinating insects away from the plants. She thinks that way, the people who buy her flowers will not get hold of seeds and so will have to look

Veruche, a wild relative of the commercially grown marigold, is considered to be the Flower of the Dead in the villages. It blooms profusely in late October and early November.

elsewhere for something to grow. She also complains that the noncommercial grow-ers are driving the price of her flowers down thus making it even harder for her to make a living.

Candles

Candles provide the smoke that allows the dead to enjoy the feast on the *ofrenda* or the light to allow the dead to see how to get home to earth and back again to the afterworld (depending on your point of view). They are an essential part of the cel-ebration and as such are in great demand during the Day of the Dead season.

Velas are taper candles under 30 centimeters high. Usually they are white or yel-low with a colored ribbon wrapped around it in a spiral fashion. *Cerillas* are similar to *velas* in that they are tapers with one significant difference. They are large, usually measuring between 50 and 150 centimeters in length. Occasionally, they are used on the floor beside or in front of an *ofrenda* or at the grave but they are generally reserved for the more well-to-do upper and upper-middle classes, as they are quite expensive. *Veladoras* are candles that are commonly used on the *ofrendas* and at the graves because they will continue to burn even in a moderate breeze. They are made by placing a wick in the center of a drinking glass or some other suitable clear container and then filling the container with wax. Sometimes, they are made in paper cups with a company brand name printed on them. Many families purchase the drinking glasses (usually with a religious saying or picture imprinted on them) wholesale and make the *veladoras* that they then sell at the markets or on the streets.

Papel Picado (Tissue paper cutouts with Day of the Dead themes). These examples adorn an ofrenda set up at a gallery, La Mano Magica, in downtown Oaxaca.

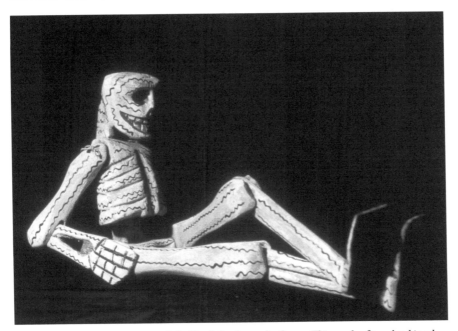

Skeletons have been the Oaxacan symbol of death for thousands of years. This wooden figure has hinged joints and is used as a child's toy.

5. Preparation

$\mathbf{M}$any Oaxaqueñans begin thinking and talking about the Day of the Dead months in advance, but actual preparations do not start until the last week in October. Some people use the celebration as an excuse to undertake major tasks such as house painting. Others signal the start of their preparations with a visit to the market. They will purchase new pots, pans, and/or dishes for use in the food preparation and the serving. Their choice is limited only by the amount of money they have and are willing to spend. One family in Ocotlán purchased a full set of eight place settings and a large clay pot for cooking *mole* while another in Ejutla only bought two new plastic plates. In addition to dishes, some of the women purchased new table cloths at this time or they will get the banana leaves to be used for the tamales. Other bulk foods such as *manzanitas* and *panela* are also bought,

A campesino leaves the market in Ejutla with an armload of marigolds and some sugar cane. He will use both to construct the arch that will frame his family's ofrenda.

although they will not be used for a few days. At the same time that activity increases in the market, the cemetery is also experiencing an upsurge. People inspect the graves of their loved ones, pruning or weeding as needed. Headstones and markers are washed. Concrete tomb covers, mausoleums, and decorative iron fences are cleaned and, if necessary, repainted. There is a palpable feeling of excitement everywhere. Everyone is anticipating a wonderful time, partly because their deceased relatives are coming for a visit and partly because many of their living relatives are also coming home.

The Living Arrive

On October 30th, the first of the living guests begin to arrive. Those who live furthest away arrive first while those who live close by tend to wait until October 31st. For example, Estela's sister who lives in Puerto Vallarta arrived on the 30th while both Fanny and Alia, Estela's daughters who live in Oaxaca (ninety minutes away), invariably arrive after dark on the 31st. They are expected and there are few formalities observed. The visitors settle in and are soon actively involved in the preparations. The atmosphere is relaxed and casual.

In the days before the celebration, the visitors stay close to the homes they are visiting but they are no means isolated. For example, on October 31, 1995, Estela's house, normally containing four people (Estela, her son, Rudolfo, his wife, Cris, and Estela's grandson), was filled with those four plus Estela's two daughters, Fanny and Alia, their children, Fanny's husband, Enrique, and my research team—a total of fifteen people. However, that was the smallest number of people in the house that day. During a single afternoon and evening, a steady stream of visitors arrived and departed. Pedro and Karino (friends of Rudolfo and Enrique) arrived around 3:00 p.m. and stayed late into the night while most of the visitors, including several of Estela's local relatives, Fanny's and Alia's former school friends, and friends of the family came and went, having each stayed less than an hour. In all, on that day, there were over eighteen visitors with the crowd often exceeding 24 people. A similar situation developed in the home of Carlos and his family in the city of Oaxaca. He told me that in the days leading up to the celebration, as many as fifteen or twenty friends and local relatives will drop by.

Of course, anyone who visits is offered food and drink and I never saw anyone refuse. Steaming bowls of hot chocolate and *pan de muertos* are served. Interestingly, during this time, neither the hosts nor the guests drink any alcohol. If they arrive early enough on the 30th or 31st, they are given jobs to do in preparation for the celebration. Close family members are given the serious jobs—Fanny and Alia were responsible for cleaning the house—while other guests will be assigned 'token' responsibilities. I, for example, accompanied Estela to the market to buy flowers and served only as a pack animal.

The Final Preparations

The final preparations in Ejutla begin with an early morning visit to the market. By 7:00 a.m., business is brisk as many of the townsfolk are already out and about gathering all they need for the celebration. The necessary items include banana leaves, *masa* (corn flour), various spices, chicken, flowers, and fruit, and the only stalls that are open in the market are those that sell these items. The only exceptions are the market restaurant stalls that are crowded to overflowing with people enjoying chocolate, *pan de muertos* and gossip. There appears to be no rush and the elders of the town congregate at these restaurants. They laugh. They talk. They comment on the younger generation who are invariably still at home in bed despite the fact that the sun is already high in the sky.

Tremendous amounts of information are given out and collected in these restaurants. Soon, everyone knows who has arrived from out of town (and who has gone elsewhere for the holiday). Although the information on who has left town for the celebration appears to be of no consequence to most of those who have stayed, I have discovered that this difference (that is, where you spend the Day of the Dead) identifies two distinct groups within the town. Those who have graves to tend elsewhere are looked upon as the 'new' people in town even if they have lived there all

Estela chats with a vendor as she purchases walnuts for her ofrenda in Ejutla.

their lives. The long term residents of Ejutla (those who have graves to tend there) are held in higher esteem than the 'new' people. For example, almost all of the political posts in the Municipio (similar to a North American County in structure) are held by the 'old' residents and when new parents are selecting *compadres* for their children, 'old' residents are preferred. Estela is *comadre* to children in six families in Ejutla and has served in the government of the *Municipio* while Virginia, who has also lived in Ejutla all her life (and who is the wife of a doctor), has not yet been asked to become a *comadre*.

Invitations are issued and plans for the celebration are discussed. I overheard one such conversation that conveyed much with regard to the Ejutla attitude towards death. Sonia, who is in her late eighties, was complaining about her daughter's lack of ability in the kitchen. Her friend picks up the discussion:

"She was always that way. What can you do with her?"

"Pah, I can do nothing with her. She is a grandmother herself now and she is useless. She refuses to learn how to make *manzanitas dulces* [a sweet stewed fruit that is Sonia's favorite]. The lazy girl is setting a terrible example for her daughters. Yesterday, she comes here to visit and she brings a big jar of *manzanitas*. She heats some up and says 'Mama, try this. They are very good.' I tried them. They had no taste. They were awful. I asked her where she got them. I think she was going to say she made them but when she sees my face, she tells me the truth. She bought them in the market in Zaachila. I made her throw them away."

This lazy "girl" is in her sixties with six children and ten grandchildren. However, Sonia still thinks of her (and treats her) as if she is a young woman still living at home.

"I had a talk with her last night," Sonia continued. "I told her that this may be the last celebration I see from this side of life. Next year, I expect to be in the ground and will come home for the celebration. Right now, if my daughter buys awful *manzanitas*, I can get rid of them and make my own but when I am dead, I am going to have to eat those awful things or get nothing at all. I told her all this but still she refuses to listen. She had the nerve to say she thought the ones she had bought were better than mine"

Doris's sister, Paulina, is about to add mole negro, *the final ingredient, to a traditional tamal. On top of the square of banana leaf, she has already spread a thin layer of corn dough and placed some cooked chicken.*

Fanny and Alia make tamales while their mother, Estela, oversees. The work is repetitive and boring but the women enjoy it, as it is an opportunity to visit and to catch up on all the news.

Soledad prepares champurrado, a sweet combination of hot chocolate and corn gruel, a favorite drink for the Day of the Dead.

Two examples of ofrendas with only one surface. Both are from Ejutla with the upper one being more traditional while the lower one is somewhat more urbanized containing some non-traditional elements.

"That is terrible!" commiserated her companion.

"Yes. Can you imagine having to eat those horrid things year after year? But I think I have solved the problem."

"How?"

"I have taken Soledad [one of Sonia's granddaughters] aside and she has agreed to learn how to make the treats. In a way, she is lazy like her mother. She didn't want to learn at first but I talked her into it. You will laugh when I tell you this. I told her that if she didn't learn how to cook *manzanitas* and I came back from the grave to eat her mother's that she bought in the market, I would be angry. I told her I would be angry enough to drag her mother into the grave with me so no one else would have to eat those abominations."

By midafternoon, the market is empty and the families have begun to concentrate on the tasks required in their homes. The women are cooking. The chickens are being boiled and the *mole negro* is bubbling on the stove. As these cook, the women put the fruit and sugar on the stove to stew and begin to mix up the *masa* for the tamales.

There are two kinds of tamales and so they must produce two batches of *masa*—one plain and the other sweet. The sweet tamales are made by filling corn husks with quantities of the sweet *masa* and a larger piece of pineapple. These are then set aside for cooking in the morning. The other tamales are a bit more complex to make but all of the women in the family gather and share the work. The second kind of *tamal* starts with a square piece of banana leaf (about one square foot in size) that is covered in a thin layer of plain *masa*. In the center of the square is placed a piece of cooked chicken and a spoonful of *mole negro*. The whole thing is then folded into a packet four or five inches square and tied with a length of banana fiber. These are also set aside for cooking the next day.

The women make large quantities of these chicken and *mole* tamales—both Estela and Doris's sister's family make 200 of the tamales—and it is usually very late by the time they finish. In both 1995 and 1996, the tamale production was not complete until almost 2:00 a.m. However, the women consider the chore a pleasure and use it as an excuse to visit with their female relatives. I never saw any men involved in this food preparation but they are as busy as the women since they have the responsibility for preparing the altar structure that will hold the family's *ofrenda*, their feast for their dead.

The Altar Structure

Before the families put out their offerings, their *ofrenda*, they have to construct a base to put it on. This is usually referred to as an altar although it bears no resemblance to the traditional Catholic altar or shrine. The families are quite careful to distinguish between the altar and the *ofrenda*—which to them are two very distinct things.

In private homes, the altar is built in a prominent position in the main part of the house—usually in the primary common room. Often, it is the first thing that one sees

An example of a multi-tiered ofrenda typical of the more affluent urbanized households.

upon entering the building. However, at times, the altar is built outside in a protected area that also serves as a focus for entertainment and communal family activities. At Pedro's sister's house, the altar sat near the back of a thatched roof patio similar to a *cabaña*.

In almost every case, the altar was built against a wall or in a corner so that it was impossible to step behind it. I know of only one case, in the *cabaña* mentioned above where this rule was violated but it was built where obedience to the rule was impossible as the structure had no walls and was open on all four sides.

Building the altar structure is an exclusively male responsibility. In one case, Magdalena waited until well past midnight for her father to assemble the structure. She was aware that he was out drinking and she was not at all reserved in her criticism of his failure to fulfill his obligation. Eventually she built the altar herself (after her father had come home and gone to sleep). She pretended the next morning that the altar had been built by her father.

Generally, this altar structure is constructed out of materials readily available in the house. Carmen and Estela both use their dining room tables without any modification at all. Yolanda's brother-in-law used an old table from his carpentry shop. Debora used a 3 by 7 foot sheet of plywood and two wooden saw horses. Several families, including Magdalena's, used various wooden and/or plastic crates combined in a variety of ways. The altar may be built several days before the celebration but, as it often uses items that are needed by the family on a regular basis, the families will wait until the evening of October 31st to put it together.

Almost all of the altars had this one large surface to begin with. Some remained as a single level while others had other shelves added. Frequently, only a single additional shelf was built along the back edge of the table. Generally, it was about one foot deep and between a foot and 18 inches high. As it was usually constructed from scrap lumber, there was no standard length although none extended past the limits of the larger primary surface. Some came close to matching the width of the primary surface but most were shorter.

In addition to or instead of the shelf at the back of the altar, some families placed a small table on the floor in front of the altar, creating a second (or third) surface, lower than the primary surface. The families used either end- or side-tables or wooden crates as the bases for these low levels. I asked several people why they used the additional levels (instead of the primary surface by itself) and only one of my informants offered a reason other than "It looks nice" or "That's the way we've always done it." Carmen said that although she didn't do this, "some people have a level on their *ofrenda* for each person who is dead."

I saw only two exceptions to the rule of 'one large primary surface plus one or two additional shelves.' One was in the city of Oaxaca in the home of a professional couple who had moved from Mexico city in the late 1970s. Their *ofrenda* consisted of nine steps, the first one a foot from the ground and the last about five feet high. Each step consisted of a single plank, six feet in length, set on concrete blocks with the entire unit covered over by two plain white bed sheets. In conversation, they told

A traditional ofrenda in the village of Zaachila with a simple arch made of sugar cane stalks to which some flowers have been added.

me that they had not celebrated the Day
of the Dead prior to coming to Oaxaca.
They saw it as a quaint local custom and
adopted it to fit in—mostly with her husband's clients.

The other variation from the norm
was found on the patio in a doctor's
home in Ejutla. It had five separate levels
and, like the one discussed above, did
not have a large primary level but was
arranged like a set of stairs. Victoria, the
doctor's wife, told me that they didn't
really believe in the Day of the Dead
but both she and her husband involved
themselves in all events within the
community. She felt that her husband's
business relied on the good will of the
community and saw their altar as a form
of "community relations." When asked
why they built a stepped altar, Victoria
commented that it looked nicer than the
ones based on a table. (The patio was
near the front of the house and the location of the *ofrenda* guaranteed that any-
one going into the doctor's waiting area would pass by it.)

*Roberto and Ellie attach veruche, the rural flower of the dead,
to the arch frame of a traditional children's (angelitos')
ofrenda in Ejutla.*

The altars built to contain the *ofrendas* for dead children (*angelitos*) are simpler in
design and construction than the ones intended for adults. Usually, the altar was
either a single wooden chair with the back placed against the wall or a wooden crate.
No one spent any time making something to use as a base but always used an object
close at hand. The children's altars were small, about 18 inches (45 cm) above the
floor (to make it easier for the 'little ones' to reach) and consisted of a single level
about 18 inches square.

Once the basic structure of large primary platform and ledges was built, an arch
or frame was added to the front edge of it. Usually two (or four) eight-foot long
lengths of sugar cane (*caña*) were used as the building material. One or two of the
canes were tied to the front legs of the table or structure and then bent over the top
and tied together to create an arch. This arch then served as a frame for the main
altar level on both adult and child *ofrendas*.

Some families used wooden poles or sticks instead of cane. Two uprights were
tied to the legs just as the canes were but these were not bent at the top. Instead, a
shorter stick or pole was placed across the upper ends of the uprights and tied into
place. This created a square upper frame rather than the curved arch. Still other families opted to use no arch at all, being content simply to have the altar by itself. When

The ofrenda constructed by Candelaria in her home in the city. It is quite traditional although several ceramic skulls provide a modern touch.

questioned about this arch, I was told that it was part of the altar and so must be built but no one in Ejutla could tell me the reason for it. In the city of Oaxaca, Margarita, a member of the Oaxacan Cultural Preservation Committee, explained it this way:

> I believe that long ago, the people of Oaxaca saw the world as flat and the sky, the heavens, were like a vast tent stretching from the ground at the edges of the world and reaching their highest point at the center of the world. The sky was like a huge arc and the arch (*arco*) that is put on the front of the altar is a replica of the way they saw the world. The large table top where the *ofrenda* is placed is the earth and the arch represents the heavens that stretches from the edges of the world and rises high above the earth.

In numerous discussions about the altar and its contents (the *ofrenda* or offering), the families emphasized the fact that their *ofrendas* had not changed since the time of their parents and grandparents. Estela was especially adamant about this: "It is exactly the same as it was when my parents celebrated." Interestingly, despite her insistence that nothing had changed, in 1995 Estela's altar lacked an arch, but in subsequent years the altar in her house had one.

Decorating the Altar/Ofrenda

There are three basic elements that are added to the altar before the ofrenda itself is placed upon it: a cloth to cover the structure, flowers and plants, and hanging fruit.

Two ofrendas in the house of Matilde Torre Felix in Zaachila. The tiny ofrenda on the right is for angelitos (children who have died). The larger one on the left is for adultos (adults).

An ofrenda found in a weaver's shop in Teotitlan del Valle. Manuel's ofrenda is unusual in that it is using a concrete fountain rather than a table as a base.

A detail of Manuel's ofrenda showing a combination of traditional elements such as pan de muertos and tamales with more Catholic elements such as a crucifix and an image of the Virgin of Guadalupe.

One side of the arch that frames Elorsa Morales's ofrenda in Ejutla. Note the profusion of fruit including nísperos, lemons, oranges, apples, jicama, and bananas.

The Cloth: If at all possible, a new tablecloth is purchased for this purpose. It must be plain white or yellow although orange is becoming more common as the influence of the North American Halloween creeps into the tradition. The significance of the color white appears to relate to purity and innocence. Yellow is also significant and that will become apparent shortly. If the tablecloth is too expensive or the altar too large for a regular cloth, the family might use a white bed sheet or some other material. I could discover no reason for the cloth other than to create a neat base for the ofrenda.

The Flowers: The dominant color in the landscape that is the Oaxaca Valley in late October is yellow. The countryside near Ocotlán and Ejutla, south of the city of Oaxaca, is ablaze with veruche, a tiny yellow (1 cm) flower with a deeper yellow center with five heads. What veruche lacks in size, it makes up for in voracity. Each plant can reach over a meter in height and produce several hundred of its delicate blossoms. Veruche grows everywhere, as a weed in the cornfields, in ditches, and along roadsides. Everywhere you look, millions of tiny yellow dots greet your eye. Soon, these flowers will find their way first to the market in Ejutla and then, from there, into virtually every home in that pueblo.

In much of southern Mexico, the marigold, a domesticated relative of the wild veruche, is called *'la flor de muertos'* (the flower of the dead) and is used to decorate the arch of sugar cane or wood that frames the front of the altars. However, in the Ejutla area and indeed in much of the Oaxaca Valley outside the city, the lowly veruche, that prolific wildflower, bears the label *'flor de muertos'* and is the dominant flower on the arch and in the bouquets that surround the altars. Marigolds are also used but they serve only as burnt orange highlights in the flood of yellow.

There will usually be four plants on or near the altars. Veruche and marigold are two. The others are *pimiento* (chili pepper—both the fruit and the leaves) and cockscomb, a deep red velvety flower. Several informants commented that this plant combination was necessary to produce a particular smell in the house. The pungent combination of pepper and marigold must be strong as the spirits of the dead cannot actually eat any of the real food placed on the altars but they can enjoy the smells of the food which, according to Debora, are enhanced a great deal by the smells of the plants. Without the plants, the food would be bland and tasteless to the dead. I was told of a grandfather who picked a veruche flower and handed it to his very young grandson asking, "What do you smell?" The young boy's immediate response was "A fiesta!"

On some ofrendas, families place bunches of pepper (*pimiento*) leaves. I was told this was done to protect the souls from evil and according to Pedro of Ocotlán, it also provides protection from strangers who might give the "evil eye." Some of the women believe that on the Day of the Dead, when the souls of the deceased are released, demons and other malevolent spirits are also temporarily freed. These spirits are said to hover near the *ofrendas* in the hopes of capturing and consuming an unwary or unprotected soul. Carmen compared them to animal predators who lie in wait close to a watering hole where all of the prey must eventually come to drink. *Pimiento* prevents this kind of spiritual ambush. This use of pepper leaves is consistent with the Zapotec perception of the soul. In Mitla, a Zapotec village near the eastern end of the Tlacolula Valley, the souls of young children are thought to be poorly attached to the body (that is, easily dislodged) and since death is defined as the permanent separation of the body and the soul, mothers will sometimes place loose pepper leaves inside a child's clothing or in an amulet around the child's neck. This

Jicama hanging on an arch of Debora's ofrenda in Ejutla.

A traditional rural ofrenda in Ejutla with the arch complete. It is ready to have the food and drink added for the dead to enjoy. (The vampire imagery shows the encroaching influence of Halloween).

serves to help bind the soul to the body and to protect it from the "evil eye" and other supernatural threats.[12] It is therefore reasonable that the villagers would extend this protection to the souls of their dead, many of whom are children.

In terms of color, the combinations of green leaves with the yellow and red flowers tends to mimic the colors in the landscape but, more importantly, the veruche and the marigold, the *flores de muertos*, are yellow, the color of death in pre-hispanic southern Mexico. According to Estela, yellow is a color that attracts the spirits of the dead and brings them to the altars to enjoy the feast that has been prepared for them and placed on the altar for them. Interestingly, the altars and the *ofrendas* on them are alive with a profusion of colors ranging from the dominant yellow to earth tones, greens, blues, reds and oranges but the one color conspicuous in its absence is black, the traditional Catholic color of death and mourning.

12. See Leslie 1981: 45-46.

The Fruit: In every house where the *ofrenda* has an arch, it is festooned with hanging fruit. The most common were bunches of bananas, limes, oranges, *manzanitas*, *nísperos*, and jicama. In some homes, apples, grapefruit, or lemons are also added. At a doctor's home, I also saw a bunch of grapes hanging from the arch. It should be noted that none of the fruits were hung on the arch individually. Instead, when the fruit is harvested, whole branches are cut off and the fruit are left on them. This obviously makes them easier to hang onto the ofrenda.

Large quantities of these fruits are placed on the arches perhaps to suggest that the visitors are special. Most of the fruit is expensive and only eaten on special occasions. Bananas, *nísperos*, jicama, and *manzanitas* fall into this category. Apples and grapes are very expensive and so show up only on the *ofrendas* of the wealthiest families. Others are usually available and affordable—indeed, many

A traditional rural ofrenda in Ejutla ready and waiting for the dead to come and feast. The food will be replaced several times during the day

families have fruit trees in their yards, especially the citrus varieties. Interestingly, the most readily available fruits, the citrus ones, are also the most pungent. Only one *ofrenda* lacked the wide variety of fruit found on most *ofrendas*. It was in the home of Antonia, a very poor widow who lived in a shack on the outskirts of Ejutla. Her *ofrenda* was the most impoverished I had ever seen. It had a small stick of chocolate, a single loaf of *pan de muertos*, a handful of peanuts (which she sells) and three apples. She was pleased that she had invested in the apples. She was willing to pay the equivalent of two week's income for those apples because she wanted her deceased husband to know that she was doing all right. "After all," she said, "only the rich can afford apples."

Finishing Touches

Before finally retiring for the night—usually around 2:00 or 3:00 AM—the finishing touches are put onto the altar. Pictures of saints, of the Virgin of Guadalupe, or of the Christ child (never Jesus as an adult) are hung on the wall behind the structure or stood on the upper surface of the altar. If available, photographs of the dead are also placed on the altar. This, according to Estela, is done to remind the living of what

Isaac adds copal to the smoldering charcoal in his incense burner. Within minutes, the room will be filled with a sweet, resinous smoke.

the dead looked like and to let the dead know that they are welcome. The people in the villages may or may not add a cross to the arrangement but this is not common and only those who have converted to the "born-again" or Baptist churches do this. The members of the Catholic majority look down upon this, saying that a cross belongs more properly on the household shrine and has no real place on the Day of the Dead *ofrenda*.

Candles are a requirement. There is no set maximum for the number or type of candles but there must always be at least one burning on the ofrenda all day on November 1. One or two may also be placed on the floor in front of the structure along with a vase or two of flowers (marigolds, veruche, and cockscomb). In the center of the floor arrangement, there is almost always a single tripod-based incense burner filled with charcoal and copal.

The villagers will not usually add anything else to the decorations although those in the city and those who perceive themselves as more sophisticated that the ordinary villager (usually professionals like doctors or architects who have spent some time in the city or in Mexico City) will add other objects. These are usually fanciful ceramic skulls or tiny skeletal figurines to, as they say, add a bit of color to the *ofrenda*. Villagers do not think these figures are appropriate, as they could be perceived as ways to ridicule the dead—something they do not want to do. However, the villagers will sometimes put little toys or skeletal figures on a child's *ofrenda*. Margarita says that the children still like to play even if they are dead and so these figures are good for children's *ofrendas*. Adults do not play and so do not need toys.

Setting Out the *Ofrenda*

This final step is done on the morning of November 1 while all the rest is done the night before. Early in the morning, often right around dawn, the women of each household begin cooking or heating the foods that are to be placed on the *ofrenda*. At the same time, the foods such as fruits of all kinds, chocolate (for hot chocolate), candies, *pan de muerto*, and nuts are arranged on the various levels. The precise arrangement depends on the family's traditions, the size and shape of the altar structure, as well as on the quantity of materials being placed. Most are simply placed haphazardly with larger items towards the back and some leaning against the wall (if the altar is set against a wall). Several families did place a single row of pieces of fruit (usually apples or oranges) along the front edge of the main surface. Sometimes these were alternated with candles. The only reason ever offered for this arrangement was that it looked nice. Yolanda's sister arranged walnuts in the form of a cross on the altar saying that "we have always done this."

Drinks are then added. First, a glass of water is placed in a prominent position on the altar. "The dead are always thirsty" and water is the only drink found on all *ofrendas*. Hot chocolate is almost as common but there were a few houses that did not put out a mug of *chocolaté*. The more traditional families would include a mug of *atole*, a sometimes sweetened drink of ground corn and water. The more modern families would place bottles of soft drinks on their *ofrendas*. The flavors or kinds depended on the ones the dead preferred while alive. Only a few *ofrendas* had alcoholic drinks on

Señora Vasquez watches as her daughter places a totopo (a large toasted tortilla) onto their ofrenda in Teotitlan del Valle.

An elaborate outdoor ofrenda at the Estancia Fraternidad in San Felipe del Agua. This is perhaps the most traditional of the 'public' ofrendas we've seen.

them. Those that did usually only held a single glass of home-made mescal and only if the dead they expect to come visiting enjoyed a drink or two in life.

The tamales are steamed in large pots over open fires in the courtyards and other foods such as the *manzanitas dulces* are placed on the stove in the kitchen. Likely, this has no significance other than the tamales are made in quantity and so the pots are too large for the stove. As each of these items was ready, a small quantity is placed on (ideally) a newly-purchased plate or bowl and added to the food already on the *ofrenda*. These cooked foods will be replenished several times during the day.

The first few cooked foods to be put out, usually *mole negro* tamales, cooked black beans, and *manzanitas dulces*, are carefully placed into openings created specifically for these foods. The remainder, which could include, but are not limited to, candied *calabaza*, tortillas, and sweet tamales, is then added to the *ofrenda* wherever they would fit. Often the various foods ended up piled one on top of the other with some plates balanced precariously on top of fruit or leaning against one another. The result looks like a jumbled chaos that seems to always threaten to spill onto the floor. The Oaxaqueñans liked the effect. Julio, from Ocotlán, said:

> It is at once a feast for the stomach and a feast for the eyes. It should be just a little bit crazy and not too neat because that is the way life is.

Both Debora and Estela suggested that the total *ofrenda* should be impressive and excessive to show the dead how much the living care for them. Also, Debora added,

This ofrenda belongs to Norma Martínez Suarez, a Triqui weaver from the northwest part of the state. She expends a great deal of time and effort to create the perfect ofrenda from her region despite the fact that she lives in the city now.

Part of an ofrenda from the village of Arrazola. It is heaped with food and drink for the dead.

Some ofrendas, like this one at the Oaxaca Municipal Art Gallery, have intricate designs of flower petals, candles, and other materials, on the floor in front of the ofrenda.

"in life sometimes there is not enough to eat so it is only right that, in death, there should be plenty."

Once everything is on the *ofrenda* and the women are satisfied that it is just right, the candles are lit and burning charcoal is placed into the incense burner to start the copal. Soon, flickering light and clouds of richly scented smoke surround the *ofrenda*, adding to the "feast for the senses." The family is now ready to receive its important visitors.

Smells

Several informants repeatedly referred to the 'smell' or 'fragrance' of certain elements associated with the *ofrendas*. For example, both yellow flowers (marigold and veruche) have intense and distinct scents that are easily recognized and are strongly associated with the Day of the Dead. "You walk into the room and take a deep breath. The scent of the flowers enters your mind and says 'the dead are coming' or 'the dead are here.' It is a good feeling." This feeling of anticipation as described by Estela is prevalent in many homes. Carmen stated that "… the smell is strong and not very nice but it is one that the dead enjoy. So it is a good smell."

On November 1, the smell of the flowers faces competition as various foods are prepared and placed on the *ofrendas*. Huge pots of tamales are steamed on the stove

An adult and a children's ofrenda side by side in the home of the Sanchez family in Ejutla. Note the use of everyday items such as tin cans and plastic buckets as vases for the flowers.

or over an open fire outside. This smell of corn cooking fills the house or yard with a pleasant reminder of the importance of maize to both the living and the dead Oaxaqueñans. Chocolate and cinnamon smells are also present as mugs of hot chocolate and bowls of steaming candied *manzanitas* and *calabaza* are brought out and placed on the *ofrenda*. Copal is burned. Candles are lit, adding the acrid smell of burning wax to the olfactory assault.

At certain times, usually at the traditional hour when the dead are to arrive, copal is placed on glowing charcoal in small incense burners. Huge clouds of sweetly smelling smoke billow out, filling the room with a cloying perfume. For a brief time, it overpowers all of the other scents. However, as the copal is consumed, other scents reassert themselves—first the flowers and then the foods. Throughout the day, first one smell and then the next achieve dominance until late at night when the marigolds and the veruche once again are the only scents present and so the day ends as it began with the sharp scent of the yellow flowers filling the house.

Some *ofrendas* also have several sprigs of basil (*albahaca*) which also has a strong and distinctive scent. Magdalena, whose ofrenda contained basil, said that it was for remembrance, but it is likely that it had some other purpose perhaps related to the protection of the souls of the dead. In Oaxaca de Juárez, Agustin Conseco had much to say about basil and its uses. In particular, he maintained that it was never used or hardly ever used for cooking. He knew of no Oaxacan dish that required basil as an ingredient. However, every day, he would slap each table in his restaurant with a basil plant or two. This he did for 'good luck' and to invoke a form of 'spiritual protection.' This protection was provided when the scent of the basil was activated. The scent is contained in an oil found in the leaves and was intensified by bruising the leaves (striking the tables bruised the leaves and in so doing released intense bursts of scent). When the basil plant ceased to produce the smell, it was replaced by a fresher one. He also told me that his family used it to protect homes from spiritual attack. It could be suggested then that the presence of basil on an *ofrenda* may offer some form of protection for the souls of the dead as the *ofrenda* is essentially a table that is used exclusively by the dead. Magdalena also added that the smell of the basil attracts the spirits "...because they like it." Perhaps then, the spiritual protection is not for the souls themselves but for the house that the souls would protect.

Calaveras and Muerteadas

During the night of October 31 (and sometimes November 1), the young adults of the village wander in a group from house to house in a loosely organized *comparsas* or *muerteada* (a walk with the dead). During their wandering, they stop at various houses where they sing or chant *calaveras*, short poems about the residents of the house. The poems are meant to be funny and amusing and often just a bit insulting.

In the city of Oaxaca and other larger regional centers, these *calaveras* have been given a new form. Most of the city newspapers offer special sections in the paper for people to write and publish short funny poems about anyone they wish. Similar to classified ads in North American papers, these *calaveras* appear only around the Day of the Dead. It is quite popular among the middle class and as many as four or five thousand *calavera* poems are published in the state of Oaxaca yearly. The Mexican national papers hire writers to produce *calaveras* about Mexico's most famous people, usually politicians, businessmen and artists, which are published in a special insert on the Day of the Dead.

The Elorsa family's ofrenda in Ejutla. Smoke from the candles carries the essence of the offering to the dead.

6. November First: A Private Affair

Open Doors

On November first, all those families who have assembled *ofrendas* made sure of two things–first, someone was always home and close to the *ofrenda* to make sure that everything was fresh and appetizing in appearance and second, that the front door was wide open. I was told that the open door is an invitation to two groups of people: (a) any deceased friends or relatives who wish to visit and (b) anyone living who wishes to enter and greet the members of the first group. In past times, the second group–anyone wishing to greet the dead–was known to the householders as they were almost always relatives or friends from the same (or neighboring) village. They brought something to add to the *ofrenda* and were given something in return to place on their own *ofrendas*. Both the gifts were usually foods, often tamales or *pan de muertos*.

Everyone who visited is treated with respect and dignity not only because, as visitors they deserve it, but also because the host families could not be sure who was in fact visiting. According to Pedro and others, it is possible for the dead to temporarily occupy a living body without its host realizing it. The dead could then enjoy all of the sensory inputs of the living person. By welcoming and feeding the living visitor, a host could also be doing so for a deceased relative or friend. In Etla and surrounding villages, the *comparsas* or *muerteada* begins and ends at the cemetery. This affords the dead the

Pedro's sister scatters marigold petals to create the magic path that allows the dead to return home easily.

opportunity to "occupy" a living body, either a *muerteada* participant or an audience member, for a time, and therefore enjoy the entertainment directly rather than vicariously.

This was not a problem when all of the expected visitors were friends, family and/or neighbors. One could approximate the amount of food needed and so on (In Ejutla, each family makes about 200 tamales, an indication that they expect about 50 guests on November first). However, in the past decade or so, a problem has arisen. More and more tourists are visiting Oaxaca to witness the Day of the Dead in the city. Many of them have become aware of the villagers' 'open door' policy and are anxious to see the 'real'

In Ejutla, they believe that the dead are more easily confused than the living are. So, the magic path leading to an ofrenda is often especially thick and intense, and therefore easier to follow.

celebration as opposed to the urbanized or commercialized versions tour operators provide. I know of one disreputable tour operator who advertises to tourists that, for a fee, you will experience a real Day of the Dead celebration in a typical home. He then takes the tourists to a village and tells them to enter and enjoy any home that has an 'open door.' The villagers get nothing and the tour operator pockets the fee. Ocotlán, an hour outside the city of Oaxaca, is one of the towns that has borne the brunt of this interest in recent years. Soledad who runs a small restaurant in the Ocotlán de Morelos market told me that in 1990 she had one tourist in her home but by 1996, she had over a dozen who barged in to look at and photograph her family's *ofrenda*. Only one brought some *pan de muertos* for her *ofrenda* and yet she offered all of them chocolate, *pan*, and tamales.

Soledad, like many others, is frustrated by the tourists. Ideally, she would like to prevent the entry of these disruptive (and costly) intruders but, as she told me: "what if one of our dead has borrowed the body of one of them?" She went on to tell me that she thought the dead of Ocotlán had more sense than to get involved with tourists but she couldn't be absolutely sure. Her cousin, Antonio, was kind of slow in life and might be silly enough to try it, according to her. She and all of her friends are, therefore, warm and friendly to everyone who comes despite their irritation with the strangers.

The villagers try to be kind and generous to the tourist visitors, not only because they may be the dead visiting, but also because the dead are quite sensitive to ill will and upset. Even if the tourist is not transporting one of the dead, there may be other invisible spirits of the dead present who might see the friction between the host and the tourist as a lack of respect for the dead. It is said that they will be unhappy and cry if there is disharmony.

The Magic Path

The candles are lit, the copal incense is filling the air and the door stands open but there is one task remaining before the dead begin to arrive. Everyone knows that in life things change. Despite best efforts to maintain the status quo, people move. As one ages, one's appearance changes too. According to Enrique, from Ejutla, and Soledad, from Ocotlán, the dead are far too busy to keep up with all that is happening to their living relatives and friends. "How can a dead one know to come to this house? If he goes to the place where he used to live, he'll find strangers there. Will they treat him well? Like a relative? Perhaps not." Others have suggested that the dead begin to lose their memories of life, and so, even if there are no changes, the

Estela, who is known for her experimentation with her ofrendas, has created a magic path not from the usual flower petals but from the whole flowers, stalks and all. Her magic path is not as subtle as most.

A rather tiny ofrenda in the house of Serafín Santiago Jímenez in Arrazola. Even this minimalist ofrenda contains all of the traditional elements required.

dead may have trouble finding their way home for the celebration. The living recognize that the dead need help.

Early in the morning of November 1, a child, ideally a young girl between the
ages of seven and ten, takes a basket of marigold petals or veruche and begins to
carefully scatter the petals in a narrow band. She will begin in front of the *ofrenda* and
spread the petals to the door that connects the house to the street. The traditional
families will extend this path or trail of flower petals all the way to the cemetery to
ideally end at the foot of the grave or graves of the deceased who have been invited
to the celebration. This magic path now shows the way from the grave to the *ofrenda*
and the family's home. The assumption is that the dead can easily return to the last
place they occupied on Earth, the place where they were buried. The grave acts as
a homing beacon, attracting the dead to the right place. Once there, the soul follows
the appropriate path to the home of his or her loved ones and he cannot get lost
because of the path's magic. I was told that the young girl who made the path is usually a relative of the deceased and that relationship between the living and the dead

imparts a magic to the path. It converts the thin trail of petals into a private road meant only for those dead who belonged to the living household.

In some cases, the dead are invited to more than one house and so will have several flower petal paths touching their graves. It is said that the dead know where each

Cristiana's ofrenda in the city of Oaxaca. Note the presence of urban influences including the ceramic figurines and the sugar skulls. Also note that it is far too neat and orderly to be traditional.

path goes and acknowledge each invitation. They recognize their obligations and do their best to visit all the households that wish to visit with them.

When They Come

In the Valley of Oaxaca, the Day of the Dead, the traditional day when the dead are released from their afterlife home, occurs on November 1. At least, that is what is said, but one can easily discover that the case is not that simple. For example, the Day of the Dead is in fact at least two days long. In Tonala, the souls of the dead children arrive at noon on October 31 and remain until noon on November 1, at which time they return to the afterworld and the souls of the deceased adults arrive to spend their twenty-four hours with the families. It is said that the souls of dead children (*angelitos*) must arrive separately from the adults since they have such tiny wings and so cannot fly as fast as the adults. However, several of the traditional families scoff at this idea. They argue that the dead don't have wings. "They are just like us. They live the same way we do. What would they do with wings?"

The dead arrive and depart at different times in different villages. For example, in San Felipe del Agua, the adult souls do not arrive until early morning on the second of November. In Ejutla, they leave early afternoon on the second so that the celebration in the cemetery is over before dark whereas in San Felipe, the celebration in the cemetery does not begin until after sunset and continues until dawn on the third when the souls of the adults finally head for their supernatural home. In Xoxocotlán, a suburb of the city of Oaxaca, the souls arrive on the thirty-first of October and so the celebration in the cemetery takes place nearly forty-eight hours earlier than everyone else. Just south of Ocotlán, in the tiny village of San Dionicio, the villagers gather early in the morning of the second of November. They start arriving around 3:00 A.M. and they are at home and having breakfast by 9:00 that same morning. Meanwhile, in San Antonino, a small vil-

Young children are encouraged to help decorate ofrendas, especially those constructed for angelitos. They are allowed to add anything they wish until they are old enough to discover for themselves that only certain items belong.

lage close to Ocotlán de Morelos, the souls of the adults do not arrive until the morning of the third of November so that the people of San Antonino do not celebrate in their cemeteries until that evening, a full twenty-four hours later than the rest of the people in the valley.

In San Antonino, this is an accommodation to the circumstances that exist in that village. The people of San Antonino specialize in growing and selling the flowers (marigolds and cockscomb) used on the altars for the Day of the Dead. Because of this specialization, the people of San Antonino are busiest during the Day of the Dead (October 31st to November 2nd). The dead, realizing this because when they were alive they too carried out this practice, delay their arrival until the third when both the living and the dead of San Antonino are available to enjoy their time together. Some people told me that the Day of the Dead in San Antonino is delayed because all of the local priests are busy until the third. Others reject that excuse saying that priests don't have role in the celebration. "Why do we need a priest? No. The dead know we can't celebrate and work at the same time."

An ofrenda in the Posada de Chencho, a hotel in Oaxaca. Because it is a public ofrenda, it is more elaborate than most private ones. However, it contains all of the essential elements of a traditional ofrenda.

The Private Gathering

Inside each house, the celebration begins slowly and quietly, without ceremony. The family gathers around the table to share a breakfast of hot chocolate and *pan de muertos*. They talk about anything and everything except the dead. There is no reminiscing about what it was like when the dead were alive. There is no outpouring of grief. The conversation is the same as it would be any other morning. Of course there are a few extra people around the table. There are the living who traveled home to be together at this time and there are the dead.

Brothers and sisters, aunts and uncles, mothers and grandmothers update each other. They tell funny stories about what the newest babies are doing. They talk about jobs, about friends, about everything. They laugh and they offer advice to each

Children are encouraged to participate in the celebration. Here, the grandchildren of Inocencio Velasquez decorate the ofrenda at the Posada de Chencho in Oaxaca.

other. Every once in a while, a flickering candle on the *ofrenda* will catch someone's eye and a quiet will settle over the group but it never lasts long and the conversations begin again.

As the morning passes, people stop by. They have come to visit with an old friend (or relative) who is dead. They will give the matriarch a loaf or two of *pan de muertos* or a piece of fruit which will immediately be placed on the *ofrenda* as the visitors admire the mound of food already there. Often, if the visitor is elderly, he or she will remark on how suitably traditional the *ofrenda* is. This done, the visitor or visitors will join the family at the table. They are served hot chocolate, *pan de muertos* and tamales. The guests will eat sparingly while they chat with those seated at the table. Soon, they will leave to be replaced by new visitors.

It seems that those people who are lowest in the village hierarchy are the first to do the visiting and, as the day progresses, the guests become more important and the duration of their visits lengthen. However, the items they bring for the *ofrenda* and the food they are given do not change. The visits continue throughout the day and, as Fanny complained, "all day we sit and eat. If we are not sitting and eating here, we are at someone else's house, sitting and eating." She laughed and shrugged before dashing off to feed another newly arrived guest.

Marcelina Lazo and her granddaughter, Maricela, place their offerings onto the Vásquez family ofrenda in Teotitlán del Valle before sitting down to a meal of tamales, pan de muertos, and hot chocolate.

Toward the evening, the conversations have gotten louder, a bit more boisterous, but before it gets out of control, the young adults are sent out to stroll around the village or town where they will meet friends their own ages. Estela says that the dead prefer quiet company and that the young people have far too much energy to be quiet. Interestingly, no one drinks any alcohol that day. Indeed, most Oaxaqueñans do not seem to understand the concept of 'social drinking.' Debora believes that anyone who drinks is a drunk and respectable people, alive or dead, are not drunks.

Around midnight, most adults go to sleep and the young adults begin to return to their beds as well. Those who have sweethearts in town or those who are simply too wound up to sleep continue to circulate through the streets. Some, on occasion, will start an impromptu *muerteada* and wherever they see people still awake, they will stop and serenade. Some will wander all night returning home for sleep just as the sun is rising and the rest of the community is getting up.

Going Visiting

Early mid-afternoon on November First, Estela carefully instructs her daughters Fanny and Alia to keep the food on the *ofrenda* fresh and to treat any guests with respect. It is a lecture that Alia has heard every year since she can remember and although she knows it by heart, she does not interrupt. She nods in the appropriate places and winks at her sister. Estela heads for the door and orders me to follow her.

An ofrenda from the home of the famous wood carver, Manuel Jiménez, in Arrazola after several visitors have added their offerings. By the end of the day, this ofrenda, like many others, will be filled to overflowing.

We must pay our respects to the dead who are visiting other houses. First, we go to Debora's house as I was almost a daughter to her father and I was Leti's [Debora's daughter] godmother. They would be very disappointed if I did not stop in to say hello.

She explained that throughout life, one acquires a circle of friends, *compadres*, and others who become important to you. That circle must be maintained even as the members of that circle die. So, on the Day of the Dead, you go to those places where you can meet those old friends. I mentioned to Estela that I noticed that most of the people who came visiting her place were elderly or middle-aged. She nodded. "As it should be." She explained that the young (to her anyone under 30) do not know that many dead. By that age, they have some relatives who have died but most if not all of their friends are still alive and their social circles are quite small. These people need to stay home and visit with family. She said that as you get older, more and more of your social circle die off and your obligations on the Day of the Dead grow. "Of my friends, only Debora and one or two others are still alive. All the others are dead. It is hard, sometimes, to get all the visiting done."

We arrived at Debora's house and were greeted by about a dozen people of all ages. The two youngest, Debora's grandchildren, were playing in the courtyard. The others were gathered around a table under a large orange tree. We offered some *pan de muertos* and admired her *ofrenda*. Hers had a couple of ceramic skulls on it (given to her by her grandchildren). Debora pointed them out. "They shouldn't be on there but the children do not know better. They are there for them. The dead will be pleased that the grandchildren brought them gifts but, next year, I will put them away."

One young man sat off by himself, playing a guitar and singing traditional folk songs. The people at the table made requests for certain songs and some sang along to their favorites. Most households had a radio playing in the background but Debora had decided to hire the musician. Everyone seemed pleased by that decision.

An interesting ofrenda from Arrazola with one pan de muertos with an unusual skeletal design on it.

We joined the crowd at the table and received our hot chocolate and tamales. As we ate, I commented that most of the people doing the visiting seemed to be elderly and that there were far more women than men going from house to house. Both Estela and Debora laughed at this. They congratulated me for noticing. "Most men would not have seen that," remarked Debora as she settled in to explain the facts of life to me, with Estela adding her own comments or clarifications. As they talked, several others around the table listened in.

It seems that in the village there is a strict set of rules that govern a person's freedom of movement. Children (prepubescent) stay close to home and are constantly supervised or are in the constant company of older brothers, sisters, or cousins. When boys become young men, they become quite independent and spend a lot of time alone or in the company of other young males. There is very little restriction in their movement. Young women, however, are rarely unsupervised. Usually when they venture outside the home, they are accompanied by an older brother or sister. They are allowed some independence and freedom so that they can be 'courted' but not enough freedom so that they might get into trouble. "A young woman must think of marriage and a family. Young men only think of one thing."

Once married, the mistrust between genders heightens. A man must be extremely careful never to be caught in a situation where people might think he is being unfaithful to his wife. He can never be alone with any woman other than his wife, his sister, or his mother. The reverse is true for a woman in her child-bearing years. She will always be in the company of another family member, usually another

The Bautista family from the city of Oaxaca. The elders of the family explain the Day of the Dead traditions to the younger members (Photo by Lissa Jones).

woman. If she was alone, a man might try to take advantage of her, especially if he has been drinking.

Estela, with a smile, commented that all men think of only one thing and can never be trusted, even as they get older. "A man of twenty or forty or sixty cannot be in the company of a woman of child-bearing age unless he is married to her." However, once a woman reaches menopause and so cannot have more children, she is safe. These women can go anywhere, be with anyone, and no one will think anything of it. It seems that the older women are the most independent of all the people in the villages. Debora then said that on the next market day, I should look at the groups of people.

The Aguilar family from Ocotlán de Morelos shares lunch before heading off to the cemetery in San Antonino Castillo de Belasco. The celebration in that village takes place on November 3rd and will last all night.

You will see groups of four or five men standing off to the side talking amongst themselves. They will have grim expressions on their faces and will keep their eyes on the ground. You will see bunches of young men brashly strutting about looking at the young ladies who will stay close to their escorts but flirt with their eyes and blush at the young men's comments. But most of all, you will see us older women. We run most of the stalls. We do most of the marketing. Not because we have to but because we want to. We get to wander and visit with this person or that. Talking. Laughing. We enjoy ourselves while our daughters and daughters-in-law are at home cooking, cleaning, and being dutiful wives.

We left Debora's house and in turn visited another six households in an order defined by Estela's estimation of the dead's importance to her. Each successive stop was increasingly more formal and each visit shorter in duration. The last stop, at a house we had already passed twice on our way to others, was very brief with Estela staying long enough to offer her *pan de muertos* and see it safely placed on the *ofrenda*. The visiting took a total of about four hours but back at her house it was as if we had never left. Over more tamales and hot chocolate, we were absorbed back into the conversation in an instant.

Victor Quiroz Velasco and his family greet visitors from in front of their ofrenda in Oaxaca. All visitors, alive or dead, are treated with great respect.

Family Obligations

The families set out *ofrendas* for their dead and they do so gladly. It is something they have always done and will always do but there is also an element of obligation involved. Estela explained that the living cannot ignore the dead. "They deserve to be happy and by giving them food, by celebrating with them, we lift their spirits. They return to their village with a light step." She reminded me that the dead offer advice and assistance all through the year and ask nothing in return.

There are many stories, both oral and written, about the Day of the Dead but most of them contain one of only two possible story lines.[13] In one story line or plot, a witness, hiding in a tree or behind a rock, sees a procession of the dead as they head back to their village. The witness always marvels at the contented looks on the faces of the dead. The other plot focuses on what happened when the living fail to fulfill their obligations on the Day of the Dead. In Ejutla and in Oaxaca de Juárez, we heard several stories that resulted in illness and death for whoever did not set out an *ofrenda*. Debora told of a woman who worked very hard and was too tired to prepare an *ofrenda*. She died some months later and Debora attributed her death to failing her dead relatives. She hastened to add, however, that the dead did not have anything to do with the death of her friend.

> The dead do not do such things. They come to us on the Day of the Dead and take whatever is offered. It is supposed to last them until next year. We try to provide everything for the dead so they are happy but sometimes we can't. We are too poor or whatever. The dead are disappointed but they understand. If you neglect them, they get angry, but that is true of everyone–living or dead.

When asked why her friend died, Debora was adamant that she had done it to herself.

> I think Luisa felt so badly about what had happened that she just stopped living. I like to think that she died so she could go to the Village of the Dead and apologize in person to her parents.

It seems that remorse and guilt await those who forget the Day of the Dead for any reason. Estela roundly condemned those who have begun to turn away from the tradition. She feels that they are turning their backs on their families and will lose in the end. "They will not have the dead to help them in troubled times. They will also not be welcome in the Village of the Dead when they die. They will have to sit at the side of the road and beg food from those whose families have built *ofrendas* for them." She speculated that perhaps that is also what happens to the already dead when families stop celebrating the Day of the Dead. Both she and Debora were horrified by that possibility.

---

13. See González 1997 for some examples.

Rosita, a newly-converted Baptist, was having a difficult time with her new religion's position on the celebration. She said that her pastor had preached against it. According to him, a 'good' Baptist would not take part in such a heathen holiday. Rosita wants to be a 'good' Baptist but at the same time, she is trying to hedge her bets. She still builds a traditional *ofrenda* just in case. In her words, "if my church is wrong then I make my father and grandfather suffer without an *ofrenda*. So, I prepare one. My family is content. If my church is right and papa is in heaven and he does not come on the Day of the Dead, all I've done is waste a bit of food. I can afford it so I see no harm in it."

Given the traditional Oaxacan fatalism, Rosita's approach is to be expected. One is in for a rough life anyway so why go out of your way to upset the dead? Why should she tempt fate by ignoring tradition? Despite the obligations and the punishment that awaits those who ignore the dead, the attention of the villagers is focused on the positive side. The villagers want to make the dead happy if only for one day. If the dead are happy, then the living can be happy for that one day too.

On November 2nd, the cemetery becomes filled with flowers. No grave is left undecorated.

7. November Second: *Panteones* and Public Festivities

Outside the Cemetery

On November second in scores of *panteones* (cemeteries) across the Oaxacan Valleys–from Mitla to Mihuatlán, from Nazarino to San Martín–people gather. When I was in Oaxaca, the crowds threatened to trample the unwary as they made their way into the graveyard. Each *panteon* is surrounded by a high wall and has but a single public gate through which all must pass. Outside the Ejutla cemetery, there is a long tree-lined boulevard that is normally empty, but on this day, it is lined by market stalls, dozens of them, narrowing the walkway so that only two people could walk abreast. Ironically, the stalls outside the Ejutla cemetery do not sell flowers or anything else that might be needed in the cemetery to prepare the graves. It is assumed that everyone will buy what he or she needs at the daily market off the

Flower vendors at the Ejutla market near the zócalo on November 2. Everything one needs for the cemetery can be found at this market.

The special market outside the gates of the Ejutla cemetery on November 2. Only special holiday items can be found here. No vendor near the cemetery sold anything to be used inside the cemetery, as this would have been perceived as unfair competition.

zócalo (about three quarters of a kilometer from the cemetery). Estela explained that only the sneakiest of salesmen would try to cheat the *zócalo* vendors out of their sales: "You buy flowers, candles, or whatever else you need in the *zócalo*. Here, at the *panteon*, the market is a special one."

This *panteon* market caters to the partygoers by providing luxury items such as purses and other leather goods, balloons and toys, prerecorded cassette tapes and the like. One booth sold animal skins. Another sold furniture. None of these items are found in the *zócalo* with the exception perhaps of the prerecorded music, but the vendor had simply relocated his regular booth in the *zócalo* to the *panteon* for the day.

As one gets closer to the gates of the cemetery, the stalls change character. More and more sell festive foods of all kinds ranging from *nieves* (ice cream treats) and candied fruit and nuts, to *tortas*, *empenadas*, and *tostados*–traditional Oaxacan 'fast food' treats. In addition to the stalls, there were dozens of *ambulantes*, mobile vendors who brought the toys and treats to you.

The noise was coming from all directions. Each stall seemed to have its own music source and vendors were listing off their wares in the hopes of attracting customers. Everyone was yelling at everyone else as they shouted greetings or made plans to meet later. A quiet conversation was an impossibility. Adding to the din was the tinny sound of a carousel. Near the *panteon*'s entrance, off to the side, a midway had been set up. There were carousels for both children and adults. There was a Ferris wheel and several other spinning, rocking, bouncing rides–all full, all busy.

Over the years, in Ejutla, as in other villages, there is some experimentation with new-fangled decorations or ideas but the people always seem to return to the old and

An old woman arranges flowers on a grave in the new cemetery in Xoxocotlán. She had been sad earlier in the day but she said that she was glad she'd come to the cemetery as it had cheered her up.

simple traditional ways, relying on candles and flowers. For example, in 1995, Estela added a Halloween touch to the decorations on her husband's grave. She carved a huge grapefruit much the same way North Americans carve pumpkins. She placed the carved grapefruit near the head of the grave and placed a candle inside to emphasize the carved face. Apparently she did not like the effect, as she has not since duplicated the experiment. She returned to flowers and candles only. I suspect that she faced some ridicule from her peers for trying something different.

On the other hand, the cemeteries in the city of Oaxaca seem to thrive on change and innovation. They share with Ejutla the basic elements—yellow flowers and candles—but in San Felipe, a cemetery only recently discovered by tourists, there are a few stalls selling objects related to the Day of the Dead. At Xoxocotlán, a key Day of the Dead attraction in Oaxaca, the stalls selling skeletons made of clay, tin, wood or paper outnumber all other stalls combined. There are also a few vendors selling flowers at the gates of the older cemetery. However, I think these vendors also want to sell to tourists rather than to locals. Many times I have heard tourists exclaim: "Gee, I wish I'd brought some flowers." The vendors who would not normally sell flowers near the cemetery are simply responding to tourist demands.

Inside the Cemetery

If one anticipated a bit of peace and quiet upon entering the cemetery, he or she would be disappointed. If anything, it is even more chaotic. About two acres in size, the cemetery is a world unto itself. Originally, the graves may have been placed in orderly rows with lots of space between them, but as the town grew and aged, the population in the *panteon* increased. New graves were dug between existing ones. As families strived to keep their dead together, burials were tucked into corners or put wherever space allowed. Today, in order to get to certain graves, one needs to step on and over a number of others.

As there is no order in the layout, neither is there order in the structures on the graves themselves. In fact, the variation is astounding. The newly deceased have graves marked only by a mound of dirt and a simple wooden stake bearing the last name of the deceased and the date of burial. These temporary markers remain until the families save enough money for a permanent one. Of course, the nature of the permanent markers depends on the family's resources and tastes. Some markers are no more than wrought iron crosses bearing name and date. Others are headstones of simple design. There are also very large headstones, some standing twelve or more feet high with ornate carvings or sculptures on them. Capstones are also common. These solid blocks of either concrete or stone cover the entire grave. The simplest look like rectangular layer cakes with the lower block being longer and wider

The main cemetery in Oaxaca (Panteon General) begins to fill up as people arrive to celebrate the Day of the Dead.

A family spends all morning cleaning and decorating graves in the Ejutla cemetery.

than the one that sits on top. If it can be afforded, the capstone might be covered in glazed ceramic tile or a sculpture might be added to the basic structure.

Some families have opted for communal plots that are fenced in with wrought iron. Some also have roofs. These are the simplest of communal grave forms. The more elaborate ones contain mausoleums, chambers where the coffins are placed on shelves. These mausoleum chambers can be subterranean, accessible through a trap door in the massive capstone, or they might be ground level buildings the size of small houses.

Virtually all of the headstones, capstones, and mausoleums are painted, and there seems to be no limit to color choice. Bright blues, deep reds, and oranges can be seen everywhere. Intense colors are favored over pastel shades.

The Oaxacan cemeteries are not covered in grass as it uses too much water. Actually, there is no communal ground cover of any kind and the paths beside and between the graves are nothing more than packed dirt. However, many Ejutla families (as elsewhere) use the graves of their dead as mini-gardens. A profusion of plant varieties grow haphazardly around the cemetery. One grave was covered in thorny cacti and other succulents. Another boasted a variety of climbing plants such as bougainvillea. It is botanical chaos. In some cases, the families planted young trees (tamarind, jacaranda, and poinsettia) that have since grown to tower over and provide shelter for many graves. It is likely that those who planted the trees as saplings or seedlings did not anticipate their growth. Some trees have totally obliterated the graves they were meant to adorn and the massive root systems have cracked or shat-

Flowers cover every grave in the cemetery of San Antonino as it does in every cemetery in the region.

tered several headstones or capstones and pushed others aside. Some of the cap-stones are heavily canted, forced to lean by the invasive roots.

Adding to this riot of color and shape are the people of Ejutla, thousands of them. Some are dressed in their finest clothes while others appear to have arrived directly from their fields. Three-piece suits and classy dresses share the space with aprons and *rebozos* (shawls). Some of the women are in traditional costumes—brightly colored *huipiles* over black dresses. No one comments on how others are dressed. All are simply pleased that everyone is there.

People have buckets, chairs, vases, brooms, bundles of food, and a profusion of flowers as they prepare to decorate the graves of their loved ones. All of the heavy cleaning, plant trimming, and, if necessary, repainting has been done over the past week. All that needs adding is the final touches. The grave is swept and washed using water collected from a central fountain. Estela and Alia spent almost two hours scrubbing and cleaning the tomb of Estela's husband. This, as far as can be deter-mined, is the responsibility of the women. The men, if they come to the cemetery and many, like Estela's son Rudolfo, never do, are responsible for building any frames required for the decorations.

Cleaning is followed by decorating. Some families simply place bundles of flow-ers, usually veruche and/or marigold, on the grave and leave it at that. Others arrange them carefully in vases. The most elaborate decorations consist of arches built of bamboo strips or sugar cane stalks and then covered with flowers. One fam-ily constructed a double arch across the top of the grave. It took them about an hour, but from their perspective it was well worth the effort.

The final touch is the addition of candles which are lit and allowed to burn even though it is bright and sunny in the cemetery. Estela commented that it was night for the dead and so they needed to see where they were going. If a family has more than one grave, and most do, they will complete one—both cleaning and decorating—before moving on to the next. The senior members of each family do the organizing while the younger ones do the grunt work of hauling water and lugging large bundles of flowers.

The people of Ejutla are conservative in their approach to the preparations and decorations in the cemetery, but other cemeteries, especially those close to the city of Oaxaca, go further. Of course, some of the graves in the city cemeteries are decorated simply with bunches of flowers, marigold petal crosses, and one or two *veladores* (short candles in glass or paper containers). Other tombs are elaborately decorated in several different ways. In Xoxocotlán for example, many of the people create paintings using multicolored or painted sand. Usually covering the entire burial plot (and often ringed with blossoms and candles), these paintings depict religious themes (Jesus Christ or the Virgin Mary), or are portraits of the individuals buried in the tombs. In one case, a man was so proud of the portrait of his grandmother that he encouraged everyone who passed by to take a photograph.

In the cemetery in San Felipe del Agua, instead of using sand, flowers are used. One grave was completely covered in a single layer of marigold flower heads. Near the center of this yellow carpet was a heart of red flowers touching a cross of white flowers. At another grave, the family had drawn the desired picture (a portrait of the

People gather in the cemetery of San Lorenzo Cacaotepec to visit with their dead relatives and friends.

deceased) on paper and then placed the sketch on the grave. When we went by, they were busy placing flower heads of the appropriate colors onto the drawing. They were doing a kind of paint-by-number project in flowers.

In addition to these incredibly elaborately-decorated tombs, there were others that used ceramic skeletal figurines, clay skulls and huge taper candles up to a meter tall (*cerillas*). The *flor de muertos* (marigold) has become only one of the design elements rather than the dominant one—as it still is in the towns and villages like Ejutla de Crespo.

It seems that in Ejutla, people plan to have all of the decorating done by around noon and there is a subtle change at about that time. Peoples' focus shifts away from the graves and towards what is happening around them. Food hampers appear seemingly out of nowhere and everyone has a snack. Food and drink vendors arrive as if summoned. Laughter is heard from every quarter. As they did in their homes the previous day, the family members gather. A few families brought portable radios or cassette players for music, but others hire the roving bands of musicians to play a few favorite songs. There are also a number of lay preachers willing to offer blessings for a few pesos. Some families use the grave's capstone as a table and set up tiny chairs for the elderly to use. Others use the capstone as a seat or merely seat themselves on the ground. There is always something to eat and something to talk about. Soon, visitors drop by to pay their respects and to chat. Again, like the day before, the dead are not discussed. Instead they are included in the conversation. Unlike November first, no one brings offerings and the visitors are not fed at the gravesite. It should be noted that at this point, the *ofrenda* in the home is still being replenished and someone from the family is at home to receive visitors—alive or dead.

The rest of the day passes with pleasant conversation, mutual visitation, and general camaraderie. It is an opportunity to visit and be visited, and that is enjoyed immensely. Children, who have little patience for leisurely chatting, run and play among the graves. When they get bored or tired, they return to their mothers or grandmothers who feed them, fix a little bed for them, or give them special games to play. Particular favorites are *el Ancla* (the anchor) and *la Oca* (the goose). These games are rarely played except on this one day of the year.

Some villagers do not arrive in their respective cemeteries until late in the day, choosing instead to extend the private family time in the home for a second day. At these cemeteries, much of the celebration takes place in the dark. The net result of this shift from day to night is to make the celebration somewhat more raucous. For example, in Ejutla with its daytime celebration usually has about three or four musical trios strolling and playing. San Felipe, where they celebrate at night, has six to eight bands, some of which are brass bands with up to a dozen musicians in each group. The nighttime celebrations are close parallels to the daytime ones in that everyone is visiting and being visited. Everyone is eating and talking and laughing. However there are some additional elements such as fireworks, readily available in stalls set up just outside the gates. These are used mostly to amuse the children

The graves are cleaned of weeds and debris before flowers are placed on them. Often, the most senior members of the family assume this responsibility.

In San Lorenzo, a woman struggles with a wheelbarrow full of marigolds.

As the sun goes down, people begin to gather in the Xoxocotlán cemetery.

although the sound and the light from the fireworks serve as a constant background for everything else that is going on.

The most significant difference between the daytime and nighttime versions is the presence of alcohol in abundance at the nighttime celebration. In San Felipe for instance, all men who entered the grounds were immediately offered a glass of homemade mescal, a particularly potent and nasty concoction. Everywhere one looked, there were small groups of men huddled together drinking. For the most part, they were quiet and unobtrusive but as the evening wore on, the situation changed. A few of the intoxicated men began to argue and tempers flared. The potential for violence existed, but the women moved in to prevent it from becoming a reality. In one case, two sisters stepped in front of their brother who was becoming quite belligerent. They led him to the family's gravesite and gave him food. They manipulated him with gentle coaxing and convinced him that he really wanted to be with the family for a time rather than with the other drinkers. Leti, one of the sisters, told me afterwards that when men drink, they get stupid and it is up to the women in the family to control him: "How he acts reflects on the whole family. To fight on this day is no good so we who do not drink [meaning the women] make sure no fights start."

It seems that for men, drinking alcohol is an integral part of any and all public celebrations that take place at night in the state of Oaxaca. The Day of the Dead is no exception. There is no explanation for this other than, as Leti put it: "That is what men do. They drink."

Olvidados—The Forgotten Ones

In almost every cemetery there is a marker, a shrine, or simply a designated spot dedicated to the *olvidados* (the forgotten ones)–the dead who no longer have any living relative or friend to tend their grave. Most people who come to the cemetery in Ejutla place one or two flowers on the *olvidado* marker and some light a candle

Traditionally when a person dies, a mat of sand is placed at the foot of his or her bed for a period of nine days. Some mats are simple while others are quite elaborate. Some artisans, like Miguel Avendaño of Arrazola, recreate these sand mats on top of graves. They use colored sand to reproduce various images such as the Virgin of Guadelupe.

as well. Often, the forgotten ones' place is the most profusely decorated spot in the cemetery.

In addition to placing flowers on a designated spot for the forgotten ones, some villagers go to considerable lengths to make sure that on November second, all of the graves in their cemetery are suitably decorated. In one village, a group of women formed an unofficial committee, raised money through donations to buy flowers, and assumed the responsibility of decorating the abandoned graves. In Ejutla, the effort is not organized but is nonetheless effective. It seems that the people who have relatives buried near the abandoned graves assume responsibility for them. Dora tends the graves of her parents and one *olvidado*. She says that the family moved away to Mexico City many years ago and became modernized. By this, she meant

Hugo Avendaño, Miguel's brother, creates a sand painting of Jesus on a grave in Xoxocotlán.

In 1995, the city of Oaxaca filled the plaza in front of the cathedral with sand and then encouraged community groups to carve and color it using Day of the Dead themes. One group produced this political satire referring to the Zapatistas as the "Forgotten Ones of Chiapas."

A boy pauses for a quiet moment beside a grave in Xoxocotlán (Photo by Lissa Jones).

that they had forgotten the traditional ways. She told me in a whisper as we sat at her mother's grave that she thought that family had lost their way but that they would eventually find their way back. In the meantime, she wanted the grandfather (the one in the grave) to be looked after properly. That way, when the family eventually returned to the traditional ways, they would have nothing to apologize for. Carmen, who like Dora, decorates the grave of a family member and a neighboring grave, had a different reason for doing so. She said that she did not like the idea of her grandfather "living" next to an untended grave. She equated it to having to live in a rundown neighborhood.

> That tomb was a real mess for years and years–even before we buried grandfather. There were weeds everywhere and the cross had fallen down. Many people were using it as a garbage dump. I cleaned it up and had Antonio [her husband] cut the weeds and straighten the cross. Now it looks beautiful. Grandfather, I think, would be pleased by his neighbor now.

She went on to say that she is teaching her children to look after that grave as if it belonged to the family. They have adopted the *olvidado*. She also confided that she was afraid that the family who abandoned the grave would become sick or die if the grave was not treated properly. She was, in a way, looking after the living by tending to the grave.

Awareness of the forgotten ones is manifest in the cemeteries but it is also demonstrated in the homes as well. Everyone I spoke to about them insisted that everyone was welcome to share the food on the *ofrendas*. All of the dead are invited to come and visit. Dora says:

> It is best if a soul can visit their own family but they always go to other places as well. My father, I am sure, goes to all of the places he knew when he was alive. He visits the house he grew up in even though our family has not lived there in forty years. He goes to his friend's house as well. Maybe he meets with him and drinks with him there the way they used to when both were alive. Even if no one living is left, maybe the dead have a reunion. Would I want to prevent that? No. In my home, all of the dead are welcome!

That attitude was particularly apparent among the group of women in Ejutla that formed my circle of informants. They recognized that the souls of the dead needed a place to go and meet with the living and the dead. Carmen suggested that the living had a responsibility to provide as much food as they could on the *ofrendas* so that there was something for everyone. She told me of a woman who lives in another village a few miles away from Ejutla who builds an *ofrenda* for the *angelitos* even though she has none of her own. All of her children survived to adulthood. Carmen said that this woman always loved children. She had eight of her own but even after they were grown, she loved to have children over to visit, always making little treats for them– cookies, candies, special fruit drinks. So why not include all of the dead children in her generosity too. "*Angelitos* need to laugh and to enjoy themselves too."

Wandering musicians entertain a family at a graveside in Xoxocotlán.

In Santa María Coyotepec, just south of the city of Oaxaca, the people take it one step further and place a general welcome sign on their front gates to advertise to the souls of the dead that they are welcome within. This sign consists of a small bundle of veruche or marigolds which is tied or otherwise fastened to the gate post(s) about four feet above the ground.

I asked several women if they were worried about attracting disreputable souls to their houses on the Day of the Dead but they were not at all concerned. As Dora put it: "No matter what they did while they were alive, no matter how bad they were, they are always well behaved and considerate when they visit us on the Day of the Dead. They are welcome and I think they are grateful for that."

Elsewhere in Mexico, according to Carmichael and Sayer, some people construct a second *ofrenda* in the yard so that the dead who had been bad or evil during their lifetimes, could enjoy the celebration but, at the same time, be kept out of the house thereby reducing the danger to the living inhabitants of that house.[14] I did not see any kind of secondary *ofrenda* in the valley of Oaxaca and no one I spoke to was familiar with this tradition.

Oaxaqueñans are generally hospitable and generous people and it is obvious that this generosity extends to the dead as well as the living. They try to make sure that everyone is included in the celebration without exception. Part of this is because they hope that when they die, they will be accorded the same treatment by their families and by strangers if the family should ever forget them. But, I think it is more impor-

14. Carmichael and Sayer 1991.

An old man shows his granddaughter the traditional ways in the cemetery at Xoxocotlán.

tant to recognize that they share their celebration with the forgotten ones because they genuinely care about them. Ironically then, the label "*olvidados*" or "forgotten

An elderly couple shows their granddaughter the traditional ways in the cemetery at Xoxocotlán.

ones" is a misnomer, as they are not forgotten. They are the remembered ones.

The Celebration Ends

Slowly, the party starts to wrap up. Mothers gather their sleepy children and herd them towards the exit. The men collect up the family's belongings and follow behind. Not everyone leaves at once but slowly, as family after family make their ways home, the noise level drops. The vendors and the musicians pack up. The teenagers head for the *zócalo* and a livelier spot. The *viejitos* (the old ones) say their last goodbyes in silence and then they too head home to bed. It is said that the dead also leave the celebration in the same way and in the same order so that when the caretaker finally padlocks the *panteon* gate, there is not a soul left in the graveyard.

What is left behind are mountains of yellow flowers adorning already festive graves and thousands of flickering candles. The yellow glow cast by these candles (they have been left to burn themselves out) creates a ghostly but somehow comforting picture to be remembered throughout the year. The following morning, the decorations in the cemetery and the *ofrenda* at home are taken down. The Day of the

A young girl lights a candle on a grave in Xoxocotlán.

Dead is over and there is nothing left to do except to look forward to next year when it will all happen again "as it has always happened."

Four More Mondays

It is interesting that the celebrations are over by the night of November third in most localities in the Oaxacan Valley system but that in four communities, the festivities continue. On four successive Mondays beginning with the first Monday after November second and continuing until San Andreas Day, there are gatherings in the cemeteries of Ex-Marquesado, San Martín Mexicapan, San Juanito, and Xochimilco. There is only one celebration every Monday night and it takes place only once in each cemetery. Ex-Marquesado's celebration is on the first Monday; San Martín's is on the second Monday and so on. They are all related to the Day of the Dead and the dead of each community but that is where the similarities end.

There do not seem to be any common threads tying these celebrations together. The people who are involved are different in each case and the celebrations are remarkably different from one another. In Xochimilco, the gathering begins around three in the afternoon with the cleaning and decorating of the graves. This time, however, there are no yellow flowers; all colors but yellow. The decorations are not elaborate and other than two small groups of wandering musicians and one or two flower vendors, there are no people there to sell the participants anything. The celebration is subdued and by nightfall, the people have all gone home and the cemetery is locked up. Compare this with the party at San Martín where the organizers have set up a stage and the grave decorations are elaborate and bright with lots of candles. As dark falls, the salsa band begins to play. Fireworks appear in the skies all around the graveyard. There are dozens of vendors selling everything one might want from flowers to candy and alcoholic drinks. The hundreds of participants dance, sing, and have a loud and happy time in the cemetery until the early morning hours of the next day. It is as raucous a celebration as the Xochimilco one is quiet. These two gatherings are as different as night and day (literally).

Accidentados

Everyone that I spoke to agreed that every soul undertakes a journey before it reaches its final resting place. One informant suggested that in a violent, accidental death, the soul is sometimes shattered into several pieces. If that is the case, the pieces are scattered in several locations—at the site of the accident, in the cemetery, and in the family home. The soul's journey is thus made more arduous as it must literally pull itself together before the first step can be made.

The living do what they can to assist the accident victim's soul. They begin their helping first by placing a marker at the place where the person died. This marker can be a simple metal cross hammered into the ground by the side of the road (or nailed to the nearest lamppost on a city street) or it can be a large concrete structure containing a niche and supporting a large metal or concrete cross several feet high.

On the first anniversary of a violent accidental death, the immediate family places flowers and a candle at the base of the marker. The flowers this first time can be almost any available type but the preference seems to be for white lilies or multicolored bouquets of mixed flowers. The candles are always *veladoras* (candles in glass containers), which are left burning by themselves when the family leaves the location.

Every year following that first anniversary, on the same day as they visit the cemetery to decorate the graves for the Day of the Dead, the family returns to the marker to place flowers and to light one or two new *veladoras*. This time, the flowers are *flores de muertos* (veruche and marigolds). Those families whose markers were very close to the city of Oaxaca added one or two cockscomb flowers. Sometimes a short prayer is offered, but usually the family silently watches the marker

and its decoration for a few minutes before returning to the cemetery. Carmichael and Sayer note that in other locations, the visit to the markers is done on October 28.[15] This is not the case in the Oaxaca Valley, although Elvia from Zaachila told me that the ones who died in accidents came to visit on October 29. In 1997, we observed eleven families decorating the markers on November second.

When asked why they decorated the roadside markers as well as the *ofrendas* in the home and the grave in the cemetery, my informants stated that it was necessary to do so for at least several years after the death. Margarita whispered that the soul, at least the fragment that was lost at the place of death, needed strength to find its way to the cemetery. The strong scent of the flowers

A tiny roadside accidentado shrine in Arrazola marks the location where someone died accidentally.

15. Carmichael and Sayer 1991.

The celebration is in full swing at the older cemetery in Xoxocotlán. The festivities will continue throughout the night.

carried into the otherworld by the smoke from the candle infused the soul with the necessary energy.

As we were having this conversation outside a *tienda* (a small store), we were joined by an old neighbor lady who reminded Margarita to make sure she told me that it would only work if the same hand lit the candles in all of the relevant offerings—at the marker, at the grave, and on the *ofrenda*. The soul fragment could then locate its own grave and *ofrenda* (and so its own fragmented parts). If different people lit the candles in the different places, the soul would become confused and unable to make the necessary connections, making the journey to its final home much longer and more difficult.

I asked the old woman if the soul fragment always eventually meets up with its counterparts to become whole again. She responded with a little laugh and the following story told to her as a little girl by her grandmother:

> Long ago, an oxcart loaded with corn killed a great uncle of mine. The fool had gotten drunk and was sleeping in the road. It was dark and a young man, a cousin, was hurrying home after a long day in the fields. He didn't see my grandfather's brother until after the ox had trod on him and the cartwheel had run over him.
>
> My grandmother and my grandfather put a cross there and put flowers there every year.
>
> Only a year after my great uncle died, my grandfather died too but peacefully in his bed. So grandmother had two graves to look after as well as my great uncle's marker on the road.

The candlelight casts an almost mystical glow over the Xoxocotlán cemetery on November 2.

My grandmother was a slow woman, always getting things wrong. (She had always had my grandfather to put things right again but he was dead now). Every year, she would light the candle at the marker, then at her husband's grave and then at her uncle's grave or she'd visit the marker last but light the candle at her husband's grave second. For three years she did it this way.

Finally, as one Day [of the Dead] approached, grandmother, an old woman, worked very hard at preparing the tamales, at cooking the *manzanitas* and getting the *ofrenda* ready. It was late at night by the time she finished. She fell asleep in her chair soon after her work was all done. In a dream, grandfather, her husband, appeared to her. He was all hunched over as if carrying a heavy burden.

"Look, silly woman! I am tired. For many years, I have had to carry this piece of Lozario (my great uncle) and it is quite heavy. What's more, it is your fault. Tomorrow, at the cemetery, after you have come from the marker, light Lozario's candle before mine. He needs this bit of soul and I already have enough."

She did as her husband had asked and from then on, according to grandmother, all of the candles burned brighter than before.

As she told her story, several other women coming from the market joined us. They too had similar stories with a similar theme—the living had to help those who had died suddenly in accidents to "pull themselves together" and that the living had to be careful while doing so. Perhaps the piece of the soul that is stuck at the place where the person died uses the living human who lights the candle as a form of transport as the dead can occupy a living body for a short time and thus be taken from place to place. However, when the rituals are not carried out correctly (that is, when the candles are lit out of order), the piece of the soul gets deposited in the wrong place.

8. The Roots of the Day of the Dead

A Religious Paradox

The Day of the Dead is ostensibly a Catholic celebration for the people of Oaxaca who identify themselves strongly with the Catholic church. However, the church does not identify itself with nor does it support the celebration as a Catholic event. Occasionally, individuals within the church will attempt to participate but they do so without the sanction of their superiors. For example, in 1995, Father Rodriguez held a mass for the dead on November second in the open-air chapel in the Ejutla cemetery. That mass was well attended but the participants perceived it as separate from the Day of the Dead and many felt it competed with or interfered with the celebration. Margarita and Carmen both complained that "… the mass [held at noon] made us wait here for an extra hour. The fountain was empty so there was no

Only a few people showed up for the Day of the Dead Mass in the evening of November 1 in the church in Soledad Etla.

A woman praying in the mausoleum in the San Antonino cemetery.

water for washing the tombs. The water truck couldn't come and fill the fountain while the mass was going on. So we waited."

When I asked Margarita why she had attended the mass, she replied that she had to. There was nothing else that could be done while it was going on and to have done otherwise would have been disrespectful. This sentiment was echoed by many of the people who attended the mass. The only people who did not attend the mass were those whose family plots were far enough away from the chapel that they could ignore the mass without being overtly disrespectful. Estela, whose family's grave is within a few feet of the chapel, did not attend or participate in the mass but she did sit quietly on one of the tombs through the entire service. Throughout, she was clearly impatient to get back to the cleaning and decorating. She asked me for the time every few minutes and occasionally exchanged glances with Fanny, her daughter, who was sitting beside her. Later, she vocalized her feelings: "That chapel is for praying, in private, not for mass. The priest should have waited until all the work was done before he said mass. An evening service in the church would have been better."

The Padre admitted that holding the mass in the cemetery had not had the effect he'd hoped for:

> In the Church, *todosantos* [including both All Saints' and All Souls' days] is a time to remember and to pray for the souls of those who have gone before. Since coming to Ejutla, I have realized that the Day of the Dead is more important to the people than *todosantos.* Many times, I offer a mass for the dead in the church but few people come. They say they are too busy in the cemetery. So, I think to myself, why not go to them. We have a nice chapel there. So I do. People come but no one prays for the dead. They come out of respect for me and the church, not for any other reason. Not to remember the dead as they should.
>
> Afterwards, I hear many people complain–in a nice way. One woman says to me: "The cemetery is too hot for you in your robes. You need to say mass in the cool church." [he laughs] I think she was telling me to stay where I belong.

A large representation of the rain god "Cocijo" at Lambityeco, an archaeological site east of the city of Oaxaca (photo by Ellie Braun-Haley).

The archaeological site of Yagul. A typical town that existed before the arrival of the Spanish.

Clearly, the townsfolk make a distinction between All Souls' and All Saints' Days and the Day of the Dead. So does the Catholic church. I spoke to a number of people at the Archdiocese about the church's involvement with and position concerning the Day of the Dead. One official chose these words with great care:

> *Todosantos* is an important celebration in the Church calendar. We would like all of our parishioners to observe it. However, the Day of the Dead is quite different. The Archdiocese has no official position on this holiday. It is not part of our calendar and we have nothing to do with it.

This suggests to me that the Spanish were not entirely successful in eradicating the indigenous religion and the result is a paradox. On one hand, there is the Catholic church rejecting the Day of the Dead as a religious celebration and on the other, there are devout Catholics insisting, as Luis put it: "… the Day of the Dead is the Catholic celebration of the year."

The villagers do not see the paradox nor do they perceive of any need to reconcile it, but this apparent paradox assumes tremendous importance as it relates directly to the Oaxacan attitudes towards death in general and to their dead in particular. I suspect that the paradox can be resolved by looking at the roots of the celebration that clearly predate the arrival of the Spanish conquistadors and their religion.

The Spiritual Conquest

The spiritual conquest of the indigenous people of Oaxaca began in 1528 with the arrival of friars of the Order of Santo Domingo (the Dominican Order).[16] Other orders soon followed and between 1529 and 1670 (a scant 142 years), forty-eight monasteries were constructed in the Oaxaca area to bring the word of God to the natives.[17]

This religious conquest was inevitable given the doctrines in place during the 1400s and 1500s that

> ... religious infidelity ... was regarded ... as a sin to be punished with fire and fagot in this world, and eternal suffering in the next.... Under this code, the territory of the heathen, wherever found, was regarded as a sort of religious waif, which, in default of a legal proprietor, was claimed and taken possession of by the Holy See.[18]

In an effort to wipe out the 'pagan' religion of the Oaxaqueñans, the conquistadors destroyed the temples and pyramids and used the stone to build Catholic churches like this one in the town of Mitla east of the city of Oaxaca.

The fact that the conquest was as successful as it was cannot be attributed entirely to religious fervor on the part of the friars, monks, and priests, nor can it be attributed to the superior military might of the conquerors. Rather, it was successful in large part because of the attitudes of the indigenous peoples and the high degree to which the Catholic religion and that of the indigenous people paralleled one another.

16. Instituto de Estádistica Geografia e Informática 1993: 18-19; García Martínez 1997: 59.
17. Andrews and Hassig 1984: 4; also see Braden 1930; Gerhard 1972.
18. Prescott 1994: 256-257.

A carved stone figure from the site of Monte Alban. The face in the stomach is said to represent the soul of the individual in this carving.

Although the cross and the candle are thought to be Catholic symbols, they are not. They were part of the Zapotec set of symbols long before the Spanish arrived.

This ofrenda combines both prehispanic and colonial elements but it also mixes Oaxacan regions as there are elements from both the Central Valley and the Coastal areas.

Three key prehispanic symbols – incense, a candle, and yellow flower petals – are all combined on the floor in front of an ofrenda in the village of Arrazola. The bar of soap was added to this arrangement by one of the young children in the family and so was not part of the original design for the ofrenda.

Detail of the facade of the Church of Saint Francis in Oaxaca. This figure holds a skull, a symbol for death held both by the Catholic and Prehispanic religions.

Torn posters on a Oaxacan wall. From the expressions on the skeletal faces, these posters appear to have advertised some public Day of the Dead event.

The cross, like the skull, is a symbol used by both the Catholic Church and the Prehispanic religion.

As William Prescott noted, there were some striking similarities between the Roman Catholic church and the indigenous religion. Conversion was more a change of labels than of beliefs.

> It is only required of him [the savage] to transfer his homage from the image of Quetzalcoatl, the benevolent deity who walked among men, to that of the Virgin or the Redeemer; from the Cross, which he has worshipped as the emblem of the god of rain, to the same cross, the symbol of salvation.[19]

Prescott was not the first to remark on these similarities. Toribio de Benaventi (Motolía), a Franciscan friar who arrived in 1524, suggested that the indigenous people were predisposed to the Church before the conquest.[20]

Whatever religion the Zapotec had, the Spanish tried to destroy and to replace it with Catholicism. They were not completely successful. As Madsen notes "... the Indians frequently made offerings to images of Catholic saints and pagan gods placed side by side on their home altars."[21] Indeed, the indigenous people turned the Spanish efforts at destruction into positive reinforcement for their prehispanic religions. The Spanish smashed the 'pagan' idols and used them to build the new churches. This was interpreted by the natives as an indication that "... their gods were so strong, that they were put as foundations and cornerstones of the temples."[22]

Symbolism and Prehispanic Roots

The prehispanic celebration has melded with the Catholic fiesta to create a unique annual event rife with double meanings. For example, many of the prehispanic gods are now associated with Catholic saints—not replaced by but associated with them. Place names tell us this indirectly. Chantutl was the prehispanic god of journeys. St. Christopher (San Cristobal in Spanish) was the patron saint of travelers. In southern Oaxaca, there is a town called San Cristobal de Chantutl. Coincidence? All Catholic prayers are offered to Jesus or to various saints rather than to God directly. This is also in keeping with prehispanic beliefs wherein the highest gods were too aloof to take an interest in the affairs of lowly humans. It was the lesser gods who intervened, who took an interest. The Catholic set of saints allowed the people to transpose the powers of those lesser gods to those saints and there is an almost perfect match.

Fray Diego Durán, a Dominican friar, wrote in the late sixteenth century that the people were making offerings to the dead children and adults on All Souls' and All Saints' days. He wrote "... it is an evil simulation ... the feast has been passed to the

19. Prescott 1994: 145.
20. Cervantes 1991; also see Carmichael and Sayer 1991: 38.
21. Madsen 1960.
22. Brenner 1929.

A quaint and traditional ofrenda in the home of Maximiliano Morales in Arrazola.

Feast of Allhallows in order to cover up the ancient ceremony."[23] Despite the best efforts of the conquistadors to obliterate the Mesoamerican religions, elements of that religion survived. For example, one of the most common items you will see are skulls made of sugar and brightly decorated with icing sugar piping. They will all have a tiny rectangle of foil on the forehead. This is an indigenous response to repressive overlords. According to some early Spanish chroniclers, these pagans of the 16th century would, every year, dig up the remains of their ancestors, particularly the skull, and clean the bones, paint them bright colors and put a prayer and the name of the person to whom the skull belonged *on the forehead.* The new Spanish government put a stop to that. No more digging up the bodies of the deceased. So, the Mexican people came up with an alternative—candy skulls that were decorated with the name on the forehead and so on—to replace the real thing. The foil piece on

23. as cited in Horcasitas 1979

Another traditional ofrenda in a house in San Lorenzo.

the forehead is for the person's name. Incidentally, in the city, the people say that you put a living person's name on it and thereby wish that person a comfortable death (at some point far in the future). In the villages south of the city, the names written on the skulls are always the names of people already dead. The living are letting the dead know they are not forgotten.

The skeleton itself is a common prehispanic symbol for death. Several of the Mayan, Aztec, and Zapotec Gods of death are depicted as skulls or skeletons. Often you will see the stages of a person's life depicted in art here as consisting of three faces—a young man, an old man and a skull (death). This reflects the fact that death does not end the person's involvement with this life. Instead it is just another stage of life.

Some of the prehispanic elements in the Day of the Dead are worth noting and we must begin with its dominant color—yellow. Yellow is the Zapotec color of death and the color that coincides with the direction south (where the Village of the Dead is located). The color most often associated with death for Catholics is black.

Occasionally, there will be a cross on an *ofrenda* but it is not the typical Mexican crucifix. It lacks the figure of Jesus and that absence suggests that this cross has prehispanic roots. Indeed, it could be argued that this particular cross represents the pan-Mexican Tree of Life. This mythical tree is both a support pole for the sky and a 'magic pathway' connecting the three levels of the prehispanic world: "... the starry arch of heaven, the stony Middleworld of earth made to flower and bear fruit by the blood of kings, and the dark waters of the Underworld below."[24] It is said that you can see where the tree meets the sky by looking in the vicinity of the North Star. There you will see a blank spot, void of stars. That is where the tree and the sky touch.

Part of the Mesoamerican world view has the tree of life keeping the sky (the heavens) supported above the world of men much like a tent is supported by a center pole. The world then is symbolized on the *ofrenda* by the three basic levels. The floor represents the underworld. The tabletop is the world of men and the arch represents the sky stretching overtop of it all. The *ofrenda* is their universe in miniature.

Aurora Cruz Cabos states that candles are important symbols on an *ofrenda* in that they symbolically light the way for the souls of the dead.[25] This is a Catholic concept that complements the prehispanic view. Traditionally, offerings to the gods and to the dead were burned so that the smoke could take the offerings from this world to the next. Likely the smoke from the candles and the burning copal incense serves a similar function on the Day of the Dead *ofrendas*.

Both the candles and the incense have another significance in that they are associated with the creation of the world. According to tradition, a god ground the bones of the people who had died in an earlier cycle of life and mixed them with his own blood to create the current human population.[26] From that time, the people have owed that god a debt to be paid in the 'blessed substance" which can be many things:

> the milk of an animal or a human; *the sap of a tree, especially copal,* the resin used as incense; it is the sweat from a human body, tears from a human eye, *the melted wax dripping down the side of a candle,* the rust on metal.[27]

I have no doubt that the majority of the people of southern Mexico are Catholic and they would ardently deny the pagan basis for the Day of the Dead, but at the same time, by separating it a bit from the church, they accept the possibility that it is not completely a Catholic holiday. Indeed, I think that the Day of the Dead is all that much more powerful and meaningful because it has a strong prehispanic base plus some elements of Catholicism. Depending on your point of view, you could define the Day of the Dead as a purely Christian phenomenon, as a prehispanic event or as a synergistic celebration combining elements of both.

---

24. Schele and Freidel 1990: 66.
25. Aurora Cruz Cabos 1993: 26-29.
26. Carmichael and Sayer 1991: 25; also see Bierhorst 1974.
27. Freidel, Schele and Parker 1993: 51; emphasis mine.

The Cult of Death and the Day of the Dead

The Day of the Dead is an important celebration to the people of Oaxaca for many reasons and as such it has been written about at length. However, most of the writing has presented a sensationalized version of the holiday while obscuring its real importance. For example, Esperón states that: "The cult of death is present in all the Mesoamerican cultures. ... In Oaxaca death is celebrated. It is praised. It is embraced.... It is prayed to. It is eaten. It is drunk. It is feared ..."[28] Childs and Altman state that "a dead person's soul becomes a supernatural being with the power to intercede on behalf of family members" and so they believe that "indigenous people do not pray *for* souls, but *to* them."[29]

Leslie also fell into the "Cult of the Dead" trap. He states that "Townspeople prayed to the saints and to the souls, and it was to them, not to God, that they attributed miraculous events."[30] Further, he argues that the souls were deified and that "... the souls were more sacred to townspeople than the saints because they were more intimately and permanently related to individuals than were the saints."[31] He bases his conclusions concerning the deification of the deceased on three categories of evidence: (1) the townspeople are forced to adorn the Day of the Dead altars or face dire consequences; (2) they offer prayers to the dead usually for specific reasons such as revenge, success in a business venture or the like; and (3) people will attempt to lie or cheat the saints in prayers for assistance but would not dare do so when asking the aid of the dead.[32]

Underlying his interpretation of the relationships between the living and their deceased kin is the tacit assumption that because the dead are dead, they are no longer part of the village social system. However, I would argue that that assumption is false and so leads to a misinterpretation of the situation. If you accept that the dead kinfolk are still part of the social network, we can easily restate Leslie's arguments: (1) the townsfolk have a social obligation to adorn the Day of the Dead altars just as they have obligations to parents, siblings, godparents and others. Failure to meet any of those obligations almost always carries consequences that could be perceived as dire; (2) Oaxacan villagers frequently consult with kin or request help with specific projects and this case is no different. Those things they would ask of the living, they also ask of the dead. They ask for and expect help from all kin, dead or alive. In Ejutla, these requests for aid addressed to the dead are ritualized. They could be mistaken for prayers but they are not. They are stylized, formal requests almost identical in form to the formal petitions presented to living elders, godparents or government officials; (3) Leslie recognizes that in a market situation

28. Esperón 1997: 8-9.
29. Childs and Altman 1982; also see Lechuga 2002: 19; emphasis in original.
30. Leslie 1981: 57.
31. Leslie 1981: 63-64.
32. Leslie 1981: 63-64.

A street procession carrying the figure of the virgin in Xoxocotlán. Note the predominance of women.

one is considered an astute businessman if one is able to take advantage of a stranger but to cheat a fellow villager is frowned upon. The situation with the dead parallels this logic. You can cheat on or lie to a saint (a spiritual stranger) to gain some advantage but you would be expected to be honest and forthright with your deceased kin. It is simply proper family etiquette.

While in Ejutla, I witnessed many contacts between the living and their dead. Each living individual approached their own dead kin (always a certain person rather than the generic dead) differently depending on the reason for the contact, the relationship the two shared when both were alive (never did a person seek contact with a dead relative with whom there had been no social relationship in the living world), and the status the deceased had achieved prior to his or her demise. For example, Juanita gossiped with her deceased sister on the Day of the Dead using almost exactly the same phraseology, tone of voice, and cadence she had used the night previous with a living sister who was visiting from the Isthmus. I asked Juanita if she ever asked a deceased relative for help of any kind. She thought for a minute then replied: "Sometimes I ask uncle Miguel to help me but I do that just to make him feel useful. My father [who is still living] gives me all the help I need." Juanita continued by saying that when her uncle was alive he liked to help but was more of a hindrance but she asked him anyway so his feelings wouldn't be hurt, a practice she apparently continued after his death.

Juanita's uncle and sister, although deceased, remain within the social network and they maintain the same relative positions they occupied when alive. If they had been deified at death as Leslie suggests, one would expect all of the dead to achieve high status automatically upon death but that is clearly not the case here.[33]

Maria has three young children (under seven years of age when this conversation took place) and one who had died when he was four or five. When we talked about the children, Maria told me about the Day of the Dead when some of the food on her altar was spilled. All of her living children were already asleep so she knew that it had been her deceased son who'd done the damage. She laughingly recalled how she had chided him and "… he was more careful after that but boys will be boys, as they say." Her dead son was not a deified spirit to be worshipped and prayed to. He was her impish little boy.

Further, Leslie's own data argue against deification of the dead. A story told to him by townsfolk clearly demonstrate a continuity between the behavior and status of the living and the dead.

> Another story which circulated in many versions concerned the soul of a man who had been a drunkard during his mundane career. Offended when he did not find liquor among his relatives' offerings on All Souls', he rattled their altar with such violence that he knocked over all of the offerings which were not to the point.[34]

This childish display of temper does not fit with a deified, powerful soul but does befit a drunkard petulantly reacting to being denied alcohol.

If we accept that the dead are on the same level as the living (and not elevated to some higher status), the Day of the Dead celebration can be seen for what it really is—a welcoming of long-lost relatives into their previous home for a short period of time. If we consider that the dead are no different from the living (other than being dead), the parallel between the visit of a long-lost living relative and the visit on the Day of the Dead of a long-lost relative who just happens to be dead is astounding. The dead are welcomed into the homes as equals, not as gods or mysterious supernatural beings. Of course, special consideration must be given since the visitors are dead. For example, candles are lit and kept burning to either light the way or provide a way for the food and other items to be transformed into something that the dead can connect with. Otherwise, the Day of the Dead is exactly the same kind of celebration that one would expect when a family member returns home after a long absence. There is no evidence for a Cult of Death. Death is not worshipped. It is perceived as a natural outcome of life or as one stage in a life that continues much as it had done before but in a different location—one to which the living have no access. There is the one exception. According to several of my informants, life after death is exactly the same as life before death although sex, and therefore childbirth, is not possible in the afterlife. To Carmen, a woman in her late thirties who has given birth to eleven children (seven of whom are living), this would be a relief and she looks forward to a time when she cannot get pregnant again.

33. Leslie 1981.
34. Leslie 1981: 55-56

9. The Future of the Day of the Dead

Some Oaxaqueñans are concerned that the Village of the Dead is getting over-crowded. Too many people are dying. Estela referred to it as a kind of spiritual pollution. She is more worried, however, that when she dies, there will be no one to invite her home for the Day of the Dead. It is a legitimate fear as some of her daughters' generation and even more of her granddaughter's generation are turning away from the traditional values. For example, Mirasol and her husband Eduardo grew up in Santa Maria but now live in Oaxaca de Juárez. She still returns to Sta. Maria for the Day of the Dead but he does not. Mirasol confided in me that she felt the Day of the Dead belonged to the old. "It is for my mother and my aunt, not for me or my daughter. I can look at a map. I know there is no Village of the Dead. It is a myth for the old, for the ignorant, the uneducated."

The last half of the twentieth century was a time of great social change in the valleys of Oaxaca. As the population outgrew the agricultural land base, fewer people could support themselves and their families by subsistence farming. Between 1960 and 1984, roughly twenty percent of the rural population moved to the city or out of the state to find work. At the same time, only about half of the state's active labor force was engaged in agriculture.[35] Since that time, the number of people farming has continued to dwindle, and the exodus to the city and beyond has not yet abated. This is but part of the modernization of Mexico. This modernization, with associated higher levels of education and awareness of urban ideas, has turned the eyes of the younger villagers toward distant horizons. Many see village life as backward and limiting. They want more. As Eduardo put it:

> That is why I moved to the city. I do not want my children to break their backs for tortillas and beans. I am saving for their education. I could have stayed in Santa Maria but then I would have had to share my earnings with my parents, my brothers, my cousins, with anybody who needs a few pesos. There would be nothing left.

The impact of these and other changes are being felt in the villages. The traditional pattern of extended families working together towards a single goal—the survival and stability of the family—is breaking down in favor of small, mobile family

---

35. Instituto de Estádistica Geografía e Informática 1984; also see Stephen 1991:66.

units with career goals. Eduardo knows that his leaving Santa Maria has made life harder for his kin in their village but he is willing, as are many others, to let that happen so that he, his wife, and his children can take advantage of the new opportunities the city offers.

Other traditions, like the Day of the Dead, are also under pressure. Estela has observed that each year, it seems to her, there are fewer people celebrating in the cemetery. More graves are being left unattended. "The family whose grandfather is buried next to my father has not been here to visit him in several years. It is sad. I do what I can but it is not the same." It is a phenomenon that can be seen in cemeteries all across the state as the world intrudes on Oaxaca. This intrusion can be seen in other places as well. For example, the number of market stalls selling Halloween (rather than Day of the Dead) paraphernalia has grown enormously.

If the *campesinos* and villagers are not vigilant, the cultural pollution, as Margarita describes it, could marginalize and folklorize this important connection between the living and the dead. However, she is confident that the Day of the Dead will survive; altered in some small way to accommodate the changes Oaxaca is going through.

> The people of Oaxaca have experienced many invaders over the centuries but have kept their own identities despite it all. The Day of the Dead is a big part of that identity and it will endure.

While Margarita, a member of the Oaxacan Cultural Preservation movement, is optimistic, Marco, who works in the tourist industry, is not. "For several years now, the cemetery at Xoxo [Xoxocotlán] has been packed with tourists. I think more tourists than locals go there now." He worries that the celebration might become a hollow shell of the original. According to him, it is becoming more commercial with many locals catering to the tourists' hunger for the unusual, the weird, the exotic. If that happens, the Day of the Dead will be nothing more than a quaint folk custom to amuse the tourists and a lucrative source of income for enterprising Oaxaqueñans.

Interestingly, Marco, who sees himself as part of the problem and feels badly about it, is also part of the possible solution. As he conducts his tours through the cemeteries at Xoxocotlán, San Felipe, and San Antonino, he instructs his tourists on the history and meaning of the Day of the Dead. He personalizes the dead by showing the tourists the grave of his uncle and talking about him. He explains the importance of respect for family ties and of the need to connect with all family members–living and dead. It is clear that Marco is getting through to them. On the bus back to the hotel, there is little talk of how strange it was to be in a cemetery at night. Instead, many of the tourists lament the fact that they do not have a Day of the Dead, a way to connect with their dead loved ones.

The Day of the Dead could become folklorized, a "hollow shell of the original" for some but for many others, like Marco and Margarita and Estela, it will remain a strong and vital part of the Oaxacan way of life. With luck and faith, perhaps the two worlds, that of the living and that of the dead, will continue to meet on the Day of the Dead long after we have gone to the other side.

Mirasol's generation reject what they see as backward and isolationist. They embrace the American way of life as they see it on television. They want to be rich and independent. Eduardo is saving for a move to the United States. There are few people under thirty years of age who seriously believe in the Day of the Dead. "Such traditions served my parents and grandparents well. They had hard lives and needed the Day of the Dead and its promise of comfort after death to get them through. But we know that by going to the United States, we will have comfort before we die." The present is being replaced by the future and mutual cooperation is being supplanted by survival of the individual. Traditional village values are losing out to the American 'better life.'

Although the beliefs will soon be gone, the celebration of the Day of the Dead will continue. Indeed, it may grow but, unfortunately, it will be but a hollow shell of the original. The celebration will shift from the privacy of the home to the publicity of the cemetery. Dead relatives and friends will be transformed into the mythical dead. Perhaps we will see the rise of a true "Cult of the Dead" but the cult's goals will be economic rather than spiritual. The living will use the dead to feed the tourists' hunger for the unusual, the weird. The market of the Dead will grow to cater to the tourist and the young will leave their natal homes for 'greener pastures' in ever increasing numbers. It is inevitable that the roots of the celebration will weaken until the Day of the Dead is nothing more than a quaint folk custom to be amused by. Soon, the two worlds, that of the living and that of the dead, will no longer meet on *el día de muertos*.

Zacarias and Emilia of Teotitlan del Valle have tried to keep the tradition going but as the Day of the Dead evolves, non-traditional elements make their appearance on the altars.

This public ofrenda in the home of Irene Aguilar of Ocotlán contains many non-traditional elements including a Christ figure and a sand painting of the Virgin of Guadalupe. Each year, both the ofrendas and the grave decorations become more elaborate as the people of the Oaxacan Valleys compete with each other for the honor of having the biggest and the best.

References Cited

Alvarez, Luis Rodrigo (1994) *Geografia General del Estado de Oaxaca, Second Edition.* Carteles editores. Oaxaca.

Andrews, Richard J. and Ross Hassig (1984) Editor's introduction: the historical context In *Treatise on the Heathen Superstitions That Live Among the Indians Native to This New Spain, 1629* by Hernando Ruiz de Alarcón (translated and edited by Richard Andrews and Ross Hassig). University of Oklahoma Press. Norman.

Bierhorst, John (trans. and ed.) (1974) *Four Masterworks of American Indian Literature.* New York.

Braden, Charles S. (1930) *Religious Aspects of the Conquest of Mexico.* Duke University Press. Durham.

Brenner, A. (1929) *Idols Behind Altars.* New York.

Carmichael, E. and C. Sayer (1991) *The Skeleton at the Feast: The Day of the Dead in Mexico.* University of Texas Press. Austin.

Cervantes, F. (1991) *The Idea of the Devil and the Problem of the Indian: The Case of Mexico in the Sixteenth Century.* London.

Childs, R.V. and P.B. Altman (1982) *Vive Tu Recuerdo. Living Tradition in the Mexican Days of the Dead.* University of California Press. Los Angeles.

Cruz Cabos, Aurora (1993) Diás de Muertos en San Jose Chiltepec. In *Muerte Que Vueles* (T. Garcia Hernandez and R. Merlin Arango editors). Pp. 26-29. Direccion General de Culturas Populares. Tuxtepec.

De la Fuente, Julio (1965) Relaciones interétnicas. Colección de Antropología Social. Instituto Nacional Indigenista. Mexico, D.F.

Dennis, Philip A. (1987) *Intervillage Conflict in Oaxaca.* Rutgers University Press. London.

Esperón, L.M. González (1997) *La Celebración de Muertos en Oaxaca.* Instituto Oaxaqueño de las Culturas Fondo Estatal Para la Cultura y las Artes. Oaxaca.

Freidel, D., L. Schele and J. Parker (1993) *Maya Cosmos: Three Thousand Years on the Shaman's Path.* Wm. Morrow and Co. New York.

Furst, Jill Leslie McKeever (1995) *The Natural History of the Soul in Ancient Mexico.* Yale University Press. New Haven.

García Martínez, Bernado (1997) La conversión de 7 Mono a don Domingo de Guzmán. *Arqueología Mexicana* V(26): 54-59.

Gerhard, Peter (1972) *A Guide to the Historical Geography of New Spain.* Cambridge University Press. Cambridge.

González, S. (1997) *Cuentos de el Día de los Muertos Day of the Dead Folk Tales.* González and Fukuda, Publishers. San Carlos.

Horcasitas, Fernando (1979) *The Aztecs Then and Now.* Mexico.

Instituto de Estadística Geografía e Informática (1984) *Décimo Censo General de Población y Vivienda, 1980. Estado de Oaxaca.* Two Volumes. Dirección General de Integración y Análisis de la Información. Mexico City.

Instituto de Estadística Geografía e Informática (1993) *Estado de Oaxaca México Guia Turistica.* Instituto de Estadística Geografía e Informática. Aguascalientes.

Kearney, Michael (1972) *The Winds of Ixtepeji: Worldview and Society in a Zapotec Town.* Waveland Press. Prospect Heights.

Lechuga, R.D. (2002) Rituales del Día de Muertos. *Artes de México* 62: 16-25, 70-73.

Leslie, C.M. (1981) *Now We Are Civilized: A Study of the World View of the Zapotec Indians of Mitla, Oaxaca.* Wayne State University Press. Detriot. [originally published in 1960]

Madsen, William (1960) 'Christo-paganism: a study of Mexican religious syncretism' in *Nativism and Syncretism.* Middle American Research Institute. New Orleans.

Martínez, Homero Adame (1997) Un día de muertos muy muerto en Real de Catorce. *México Desconocido* 249: 9.

Mozzi, C. Mapelli (1997) Magia de azúcar y garbanzos en el mercado de Toluca. *México Desconocido* 249: 20-25.

Newbold Chiñas, B. (1992) *The Isthmus Zapotecs: A Matrifocal Culture of Mexico, Second Edition.* Harcourt Brace Jovanovich College Publishers. New York.

Prescott, W. H. (1994) *History of the Conquest of Mexico.* The Folio Society. London. [Originally published in 1843].

Schele, Linda and David Freidel (1990) *A Forest of Kings: The Untold Story of the Ancient Maya.* Wm. Morrow and Co. New York.

Spicer, Edward H. (1966) Ways of life. In *Six Faces of Mexico* edited by Russell C. Ewing. Pp. 64-102. University of Arizona Press. Tucson.

Stephen, L. (1991) *Zapotec Women.* University of Texas Press. Austin.

Whitecotton, Joseph W. (1977) *The Zapotecs: Princes, Priests, and Peasants.* University of Oklahoma Press. Norman.

Index

Introduction

tortas, 10